A Girl's Guide to Life

THE COMPLETE INSTRUCTIONS

From The Editors of Planet D

Compiled by Susan Pohlman
and Priscilla Turner

Illustrated by Bob Staa

PLANET DEXTER®

A Satellite of Addison Wesley Longman

Copyright © 1998 Real Life Publishing
Illustrations copyright © 1997 Bob Staake

ISBN 0-201-15167-7
Cover design by Chris Sykes
Book design by Marta Rulifson, MKR Design
Illustrations by Bob Staake
Text set in 10-point Opti Beth by Vicki L. Hochstedler

1 2 3 4 5 6 7 8 9 -RNT-0100999897

First printing, October 1997

Through the Addison Wesley Longman Triangle program, Planet Dexter books are available from your bookseller at special discounts for bulk purchases; or, contact the Corporate, Government, and Special Sales Department at Addison Wesley Longman, One Jacob Way, Reading, MA 01867; or call (800) 238-9682.

And Now a Message from Our Corporate Lawyer:
Neither the publisher nor the author shall be liable for any damage that may be caused or sustained as a result of any of the activities in this book without specifically following instructions, conducting the activities without proper supervision, or ignoring the cautions contained in this book.

You can find out more about the Planet Dexter family at:
http://www.planetdexter.com

The Planet Dexter Guarantee!
If for any reason you are not satisfied with this book, please send a note telling us why (how else will we be able to make our future books better?), along with the book, to The Editors of Planet Dexter, One Jacob Way, Reading, MA 01867. We'll read your note carefully, and send back to you a free copy of another Planet Dexter book. And we'll keep doing that until we find just the right Planet Dexter book for you.

Contents

Contents by Chapter

Safety, Hygiene, and Grooming...57

Stuff to Eat ....5..........67

Fixing & Making Things 85

Things to Do Outside 189

Introduction

Thanks for choosing to read *A Girl's Guide to Life.* We all hope you enjoy it and that it gives you lots of good ideas about fun and useful things you can do to make your own life more interesting.

Here's how we found all the stuff in this book: we asked hundreds of kids (and grown-ups) for things they knew that they thought other kids ought to know. Some of them sent us their ideas by e-mail, some by regular mail and some even telephoned us. Sometimes, the information came from parents and teachers, but a lot of it came from kids just like you. We've tried to identify everybody who helped us by making a list of contributors. You'll find it at the back of this book.

If you know something you think other girls ought to know, please send it to us. We'll include it in our newsletter or use it in another edition of this Guide.

Our address is:

Kids Life
116 W. Jefferson Street,
Mankato, KS 66956 USA

Or you can visit us on the World Wide Web at:
http://www.kidslife.com

Either way, we hope you'll stay in touch with us—and with all the other kids who made this book possible.

Thanks!

P. S. The publisher enjoys hearing from kids, too—really! You can write them at:

The Editors of Planet Dexter
One Jacob Way
Reading, MA 01867

Or you can send e-mail to:
pdexter@awl.com

1. Money

Spending money is fun! But it's even more fun if the money you spend is money you've earned all by yourself. Here's how to do it.

Chores for Cash

A lot of these ideas are oldies-but-goodies, but people will pay to have these chores done!

Babysitting

Babysitting is a good way to make extra money, but just remember that it requires a lot of work and responsibility! Groups like the Red Cross, Girl Scouts, and YWCA are good places to look for babysitting classes to develop the skills you need to take good care of younger children. Once you're ready to take on a job, here are some things that might make it a little easier:

The Basic Babysitting Kit

Construction paper Markers/ Crayons Paper Bags
Dull scissors Playing Cards Rubber Bands
Tape or Glue Pipe Cleaners *Toothpicks
*Yarn, buttons, beads
A Small First Aid Kit containing Band Aids and Lozenges

Extras: Books, movies, music, dress-up

*Don't give small items like these to really little kids—they could choke on them.

Here's One Way to Wear Out Kids You Have to Babysit:

Make magazine paper dolls. Take with you some old magazines with lots of photographs—*People* is the best—which you don't mind cutting up. Then cut out figures from the magazines, especially pictures of celebrities. Cut out clothing and heads to fit the figures, making sure you remember tabs on the clothing. And cut out heads too—lots of them. That's what makes it fun. Cut out all different kinds of heads—animals, babies, whatever! Make sure to cut tabs here, too. Everyone will have fun putting different heads on the figures.

Snow Shoveling

Form a team of girls and go door to door. The more girls, the faster you'll complete the job, the faster you complete the job, the more jobs you can take on, the more jobs you take on, the more $$ you make!

You should have road salt, as well as shovels, as part of your gear.

Raking Yards

People hate raking yards. You can get rich doing it for them. Here's all you need: a rake and some leaves.

Washing Cars

If you get a crew, it will be easier, but you'll also have to share the money with your helpers. You decide.

- Make sure all the windows are closed before you hose the car down.

- Soap the car down by hand, using rags or big sponges. Always start at the top and work your way down. When your bucket of soapy water gets too dirty, be sure to dump it out and replace it. Don't forget the tires—they collect a lot of dirt.

- Rinse the car off thoroughly with the hose. Dry it well with rags.

Vacation Specialist

Let people know you're available to bring in their mail and water their plants when they're on vacation.

More Money-Making Ideas

Lemonade Stand

Who doesn't like lemonade on a hot day? If you use a frozen concentrate, jazz the pitcher up by floating a couple of slices of lemon on top. Keep your ice in another container, so you don't dilute your lemonade.

Olden Days Fund-Raiser

If you love reading about long-ago times, why not have an "olden days" fund-raiser?

At my library I found a book called *Better Than a Lemonade Stand*. It's full of great ideas on how to make money. Plus, it's by a teen, not some adult. My friend and I are going to start one of the businesses in the book, but they all sound fun."

"I found out last year that lemonade stands make a lot of money. I charged $. 25 and made $17.00. (Hint: Sell lemonade on hot days. Sell in the morning so people will buy lemonade on the way to work. Also keep a lot of ice, napkins, and paper cups on hand. Have a place to keep the money you made.) Good Luck!!"

Pick a time in history that appeals to you, and make that the theme. Have your friends come in period costume. Do some research to find out what games kids played and what foods they ate in those times. You might put on a play or stage a dramatic reading from one of your favorite books.

You can have an olden days fund-raiser by selling period foods and crafts. Charge a small admission fee for family, neighbors, and non-costumed friends.

Here are some especially colorful times in American history that would be fun to recreate: colonial, pioneer, Victorian, Roaring Twenties, '50s, and '60s. Go to the history section of your library and check out some books about the period you want to celebrate. Ask the librarian to help you find books on the everyday lives of people from that time.

Don't limit yourself to American history. The Egyptian, Greek, and Roman eras are well-documented, as well as the Renaissance and the days of Robin Hood, in Merrie Olde England.

Hanky Sachet

These make great gifts to give or sell. Tuck one in your pajama drawer and you'll have sweet dreams.

You will need:

- An old-fashioned handkerchief; one with flowers or lace trim
- Dried lavender, rose petals, or a store-bought potpourri mix
- A length of pretty cloth ribbon

Put a handful of dried plants or potpourri (sachet) in the middle of the handkerchief. Gather the hanky together and tie the ribbon around it, making a tight knot. Tie a bow.

Lavender is said to cure headaches. If you know someone who suffers from migraines, give her a lavender sachet and tell her to rest with it on her pillow.

Making Your Own Sachet

Roses and lavender can easily be preserved if they are hung upside-down in a dry, dark place. Pick roses a few days before they bloom, while they are still budding. Lavender can be picked at any time, as long as the blossoms haven't dried out. Because moisture will cause them to decay, pick your flowers in mid-day, after all moisture has evaporated from their petals.

Before you hang your flowers, remove the lower leaves and pat dry with a paper towel, if there's any remaining moisture.

Tie the stems together with string in small bunches (no more than 12 roses at a time). Try to keep the rosebuds from touching each other too much. If they can't be fanned out separately, put tissue between the buds. Hang the flowers by tying them to a rack or a wire strung between two posts. The flowers should not hang against a wall or window; air needs to circulate around them.

Helping Grown-Ups Get on the Internet

If you are good at computers, put notices up around the neighborhood that you're available to help in this area. Many adults are intimidated by computers and will happily pay to have someone show them how to do some of the basic stuff, like how to get on-line, how to send and receive e-mail, and things like that.

Toy Auction

Gather up all the old toys you and your friends are tired of. (Get a parent's OK.) Give each person a receipt for each toy.

Pick a date and give the auction lots of publicity. Put up posters.

Lavender dries out quickly—in a week or so—but roses take longer to dry because their petals are fleshier. Check your roses after two weeks. Test for dryness by gently tapping a bud. If it makes a hollow kind of sound, they're dry. If not, let them continue drying for another week or two. The length of time it takes for your flowers to dry depends on the amount of moisture in the air. When the flowers have completely dried, crumble the petals (not the woody part) into a bowl. Lavender's scent stands alone but you can add a drop or two of rose oil to the roses, if you want a stronger scent.

Note: Do not mix these two flowers together! Each has a distinctive scent.

On the day of the auction, put all the toys on display. Give everyone a chance to look over the merchandise.

Now you're ready for the auction. Stand on a box or chair and start the bidding. All bids should start with a quarter. Be a creative auctioneer—the more you talk up the toys you're selling, the more money you'll make.

Write the final selling price of each toy on the receipt. As the auctioneer, your take is ten percent. Make sure you keep accurate records.

What to Do with the Dough

Saving Money

When you deposit money in a savings account, you're letting the bank use your money for loans and investments. In return, the bank pays you interest. If you're thinking of putting your money in a savings account, be sure to shop around for the bank that gives you the best interest rate. The interest rate is always a percentage—as a rule, the higher the percentage, the more money you'll earn. If the interest rate is four percent, for example, that means you'll earn four pennies for every dollar you have in your account.

In addition to finding out the interest rate, you'll also want to know how often the interest is *credited*, or added to your account. This can be monthly, yearly, or somewhere in between. It can vary from bank to bank. The more frequently interest is credited, the more money you'll earn from your account. Of course, the more money you save, the more interest you'll earn, too!

Some banks charge you money if you don't deposit regularly and others have a penalty for making a withdrawal. Find out the bank's rules before you open an account.

What's Compound Interest?

When the interest on your money starts earning its own interest, that's called compound interest. Here's how it works: Say you have $1,000 in your savings account. If your compound interest rate is five percent, in 15 years you'll have $2,080. The higher your compound interest rate, the more money you'll save—and more quickly, too.

The Rule of 72

There's a well-known formula for figuring out how long it will take to double your savings account money. It's called the "Rule of 72." Divide the number 72 by your interest rate—the number you get is your answer.

For example, suppose your interest rate is six percent. Divide the number 72 by 6 and you get 12. At a six-percent interest rate, it will take you 12 years to double your money.

Investing

■ Buy mutual funds. This isn't very difficult, but you'll have to ask your parents to go with you to the brokerage when you open your account. Your parents can also open an account for you by computer on-line.

■ Invest in stocks of companies who make toys, games or other things you like. The prices of all the stocks are in *The Wall Street Journal*.

■ Start a valuable collection. If you are ten and start collecting things (stamps, coins, dolls) now, by the time you're twenty-one, your collection could be worth a small fortune.

■ Save money for a trip. (See "Saving Money," on page 8.)

Bears and Bulls

Here's what two kids had to say about the stock market.

"Try the stock market. If you have enough money to invest some, you could make big $$. I once made over $1,000 on the stock market."

"I am the president of a stock market club. We get a membership card, track stocks, learn how to save a lot of money, get weekly newsletters, [run] businesses and with the money we make, we invest in the stocks we think are best!!!"

2.

Social Skills & Graces

Might as well start at the bottom and work your way up:

Party Planner

Not every successful party is planned, but chances are you'll be more relaxed if you do have a game plan. Here are a few guidelines and suggestions:

■ **Decide what kind of party you want to have.** Don't have a sleepover party just because Elizabeth had one; pick something original that *you* want to do. When deciding on your theme, keep in mind how many kids you'll be inviting and whether it'll be all girls or a mixed crowd.

■ **Decide when to have your party.** Most parties happen on weekends, but remember that some people go to church or synagogue. To be on the safe side, plan your party for the afternoon. People go away on holiday weekends, so check your school calendar before you pick a date.

■ **Decide where to have your party.** If the party's going to be in your house, keep the number of kids down. No matter how big your house is, it's probably not big enough for your whole class. Outdoor parties are lots of fun, but have a back-up plan in case it rains.

■ **Send invitations.** Even if you're just having a few friends, send them invitations. People will forget if they don't have a reminder in front of them. Send invitations two or three weeks before the party. If you send them too early, they'll get lost in the household shuffle. And if you send them too late, they might not get there on time, or people may have made other plans. A week before the party, check with your friends to make sure they got them.

■ **Plan the games and favors.** When it comes to games, the simpler the better. Old favorites like Musical Chairs never grow old. Check the list in this section for some other ideas. Most kids love competitive games, but decide how you want to handle the prize situation. One way to avoid any hard feelings is to award prizes to winning teams, rather than individuals. Instead of goodie bags, have the party favor be a project that everyone makes. For instance, you might try repotting a plant (see "Animals & Plants," page 240) or making a tu-tu (see "Fixing & Making Things," page 144.)

■ **Plan the food.** Unless you're having a sit-down dinner, the food shouldn't stand out too much. Provide bowls of popcorn, Froot Loops or potato chips, for munching. If you want heartier fare, you can't go wrong with pizza. Keep the drinks in cans or boxes and have a few garbage bags handy. If you want people to graze rather than sit, serve cupcakes instead of cake.

■ **The day of the party.** Make a list of the games you'll be playing, and make sure you have enough prizes for everyone. Decorate the house and put balloons by your driveway and on your door. Prepare and set out the food. If you're having a treasure hunt (see page 22), set it up. Decide where coats and presents will go. Pick out some background music.

■ **Have an adult around to help you and to supervise any activities.** You'll have more fun if you don't have to oversee everything.

Some Party Themes:

A Spring Garden Party: Have everyone work together to plant a flower garden. Give each kid a potted flower and some seeds to take home.

A Fashion Show Party: Provide fabric and trim. Have everyone make a ready-to-wear outfit, then hold a fashion show.

Decorate-a-Hat Party: Get some straw hats from a wholesaler and provide some trim, artificial flowers, feathers and glue.

A Biking and Picnic Party: Have your friends bring their bikes and helmets and lead them on a mystery ride. The destination: a surprise picnic. Have a grown-up or teenage friend set up the picnic, ahead of time.

Indoor games: Off! On!; Charades; Camouflage; tossing games; Disappearing Man; Heads, Bodies, and Tails; treasure hunt.

Outdoor games: Tag; lawn games; Hares and Hounds; Body Language.

Party projects and favors: Tu-Tu; porcupine pencil holder; picture frames (take Polaroid pictures for guests to put in their frames); forced bulbs. For prizes, take a look at the Oriental Trading catalog.

Party Hints

■ Don't have too many activities and keep the ones you have simple.

■ If you invite one kid who doesn't know your other friends, go out of your way to make her feel included.

■ Don't push a shy kid into games and activities.

■ Find out ahead of time if anyone has food allergies or special diets. Provide special food, if necessary.

■ Find a teen-age friend or relative to help with the games. Teenagers still remember what it was like to be a kid, and they'll have some good ideas. Also, shy kids are usually more comfortable around them than around grown-ups.

■ If you open your presents at the party, thank each person for her gift at the time. If you open them later, send thank-you notes.

How to Wrap a Present

Wrapping a Box or Book: The trick to wrapping a box or book is cutting your paper to the right size. You should have enough to completely cover the present, but it shouldn't overlap too much on any side. Wrapping paper usually comes on a roll or in folded square sheets.

From a roll: Unroll some paper and place your gift on it, lengthwise (a). Make sure you have enough paper for the width ends to overlap the sides of your gift. Now you need

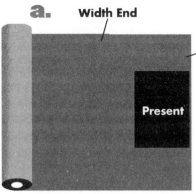

a.

Width End

Length End

Present

b.

Cut Here

Roll Over

Top | Bottom

to decide how much paper to cut from the roll Put the long side of your gift next to the end of the roll and begin to slowly turn it over to its other side. Make allowances for both ends, plus a little extra for overlapping. Cut paper from roll (b). Now, put the gift in the middle of the paper, upside-down. Bring the long sides together and tape (c). Fold one of the ends into a V shape, and bring it over the sides, to the back of the present (d). Tape. Repeat on the other end.

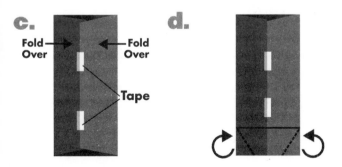

c.

Fold Over — Fold Over

Tape

d.

From a sheet: If you need to cut down a sheet of wrapping paper for your present, try to cut from just one end of the paper. Save the cut-off piece for later.

Oddly-Shaped Presents: This is what tissue paper is for! Try to keep an assortment of brightly-colored tissue paper on hand. Put your present in the middle of several sheets of tissue. Gather the paper at the top of the bundle and tie on some curling ribbon. Curl ribbon with one scissor or a dull knife. For a younger person, decorate the package by tying a ribbon around the middle of a bag of M&Ms or Skittles and attaching it to the present. If your present has sharp edges that might tear the paper, you can first lay tissue on a piece of clear cellophane. Gather and tie.

Try this: Take a paper bag and fold it lengthwise, accordion style. Make a few notches on the sides (not the bottom) of your bag. Unfold and put in enough tissue paper so that it comes out of the top of the bag. Put in the present. Tie the bag and tissue with some curling ribbon. The tissue paper will show through the cuts you've made.

Birthstones and Flowers

January: Garnet; Carnation
February: Amethyst; Violet
March: Aquamarine; Jonquil
April: Diamond, Sapphire; Daisy
May: Emerald; Lily of the valley
June: Pearl, Moonstone; Rose
July: Ruby; Larkspur
August: Carmelian; Gladiolus
September: Sapphire; Aster
October: Opal, Beryl; Calendula
November: Topaz; Chrysanthemum
December: Turquoise, Ruby; Narcissus

Gift Baskets

■ Gift baskets are fun to put together and people always love getting them. First, you'll need a basket. See if there are any lying around the house. If not, ask your friends and neighbors if they have any to spare. Check out rummage and yard sales for baskets, too. Even if you don't need one at the moment, pick them up for future projects. (Be sure to give used baskets a swipe with a sponge before using.) As a last resort, you can always buy one new. If you're putting a gift basket together to sell, though, a new basket eats way into your profit.

■ After you've collected your basket (or baskets) think of a theme. For instance, you could make a Mexican Fiesta basket and put in salsa, gourmet corn chips, cinnamon-chocolate, flour tortillas, dried chiles, and a Mexican cup or tin orna-ment. You'll find plenty of inspiration from the aisles of any large supermarket. Look in the gourmet or specialty foods sections. Always add a few non-food items, too.

■ Line your basket with a colorful cloth napkin or some cellophane Easter grass. Lay your items in the basket so they're all visible. Put in a card with your name and your basket's theme. If you're putting the basket together to sell, make a list of the items in it. Put a large sheet of clear cello-phane around the entire basket and tie it together with a rib-bon on the top.

■ It's fun thinking up themes for baskets. Your basket's theme could be based on a book—one girl we know made a *Cannery Row* basket and included the Steinbeck book along with lots of small cans filled with exotic stuff. A video, a cal-endar, a CD, or anything else you think might be fun could also be the basis for your basket. Put the gift together with the recipient in mind. If your mom loves hearts, for instance, make everything in the basket heart-shaped and include a heart-healthy cookbook.

Party Basket

These make great party favor holders. Decorate the sides and glue on a handle.

You'll need paper, scissors and glue.

Step 1

■ Take a square piece of paper (origami paper is great) and fold it into three equal sections. Unfold.

Step 2

■ Fold paper into three sections again, in the other direction. Now your paper should be divided into nine squares.

Step 3

■ Cut on dotted lines in the picture below.

Step 4

■ Fold into a basket shape: the center box will be the bottom of your basket. Fold the flaps around it, gluing them down as you do.

Step 5

■ Glue a strip of paper or stiff ribbon to the sides, for a handle.

Step 6

■ Line your basket with colored tissue paper, and fill it with goodies.

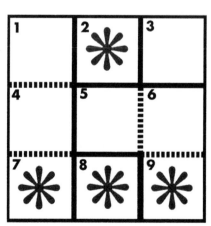

Hanging Paper Coils

These make great party decorations. Hang them from the ceiling or from the top of a door jamb.

Take a piece of construction (or any brightly-colored) paper. Round off each corner, making an oval. Starting from one of the corners, begin to cut a continuous coil toward the middle. Make the strips as wide or narrow as you wish. The closer together the strips are, the longer your hanging shape will be. Now try cutting squares, rectangles and triangles. You'll get a different kind of hanger with each shape.

Sloppy Night

The whole idea is to eat dinner without using your hands.

This gets really messy, so put a big, old t-shirt on over your clothes. Spread a plastic tablecloth on the table and put out paper plates with spaghetti on them. Spaghetti works best. Remember, you can't use your hands, so forget about knives and forks.

Put your face right in the food to eat. To drink, pick up the cup with your teeth and sort of tip in into your mouth. Styrofoam cups work best because you can dig your teeth into the cups—it's easier to hold onto them that way.

Ice cream with chocolate sauce is a good dessert choice, but so is Jell-O! Just use your imagination. By the time you've finished eating everything's a real mess—including you. That's why they call it "sloppy night."

If you want to do this more than once, you should definitely clean up the mess yourself. Your parents will probably want to eat in the other room when it's sloppy night. (NP)

Party Games and Activities

Here are a few fun things you can do with a group of girls.

Body Language

If you have a really "twisted" sense of humor, these make great ice-breakers:

Human Knots: A group of eight or more girls face each other in a circle. Each girl extends both hands to the center of the circle and takes the hand of another girl (but not the girl on either side of her). Now the group must work together to "untie" the knot they have made, while still holding hands.

Free-Falling: In this game, one girl stands in the middle of a group of girls. Everyone in the group is standing very close to one another. The girl in the middle closes her eyes, and falls in any direction—keeping her hands to her sides and her body stiff. The girls in the circle catch her and push her back to the middle. All the girls take turns free-falling.

Log-Rolling: This stunt is fun to do on the grass. A group of girls lies side-by-side on their stomachs, like a row of logs. Another girl—the rider—lies across the row of "logs," facing up. The logs begin to roll over as one, and the rider bumps her way down the row, until she is bumped off. She then becomes a log, and the girl at the other end becomes the new rider.

T. P. Tangle: A group of girls faces each other in a large circle. One holds a full roll of toilet paper. She unwinds some paper and tosses the roll to another girl, making sure that the roll doesn't break. This girl might pass the paper between her legs or around her waist and hand it to the girl next to her. The idea is to make a tangle, while keeping the roll intact. When the t.p. runs out—or the group is as tangled as it can get—it's time to roll the paper up again. Carefully, each girl retraces her steps, until the paper is wound up and back in the hands of the first girl.

A Doll and Mistress Tea Party

Marcella used to love making tea parties for Raggedy Ann and her other dolls. She'd set a table and some chairs under a shady tree and serve tea in the tiny cups of her nicest doll china.

Why not do the same? Invite your best friends over and have them bring their favorite doll. Set two tables—one for you and one for the dolls. Pick some flowers and put them in a vase to dress up your table. For the doll table, put some tiny sprigs into a small spice bottle. Prepare tea sandwiches (below, and page 71) and, with the leftover scraps, make some tiny ones for the dolls. Brew a pot of chamomile or peppermint tea, and put some milk and sugar in your fanciest creamer and sugar bowl. If you don't have a doll tea set, ask one of your friends to bring hers.

Tea sandwiches are easy to make. Use white bread, remove the crusts, and cut into small squares or circles (you can use a small round cookie cutter to make the circles). You can put what you want in them, but here are some traditional fillings:

■ Tuna salad. Mix canned tuna, a big tablespoon of mayonnaise, and a chopped up celery stalk together.

■ Cucumber. Slice the cucumber fairly thin, and spread the bread with a little mayonnaise, cream cheese, or vegetable dip.

■ Ham. Or ham and cheese. The British frequently put butter on this type of sandwich, but you may prefer mustard or mayonnaise.

Treasure Hunt

You can make a treasure hunt for one friend or for a crowd. It's a fun way to get a party going quickly, but you don't really need a special occasion to have a treasure hunt. All you really need is a treasure and someplace to hide it!

To set up your treasure hunt, write a series of clues on index cards or colored paper. Hand the players a card, which will lead to the first clue. Each successive clue will lead to the place where the next clue can be found. (If it's a group hunt, be sure to tell everyone to put each card back exactly where it was found.) The clues can be straightforward, like, "Look inside the piano bench," or they can be more cryptic:

"I have a piano
And music to play;
But I don't know where
My music will stay.
Look for a place where sheet music is kept."

There should be at least ten clues, and—to keep the suspense going—the final clue should be in code. (A simple numbers-for-letters code—like, A = 1, B = 2, C = 3, and so on—is just fine.)

Of course, you'll need some "treasure" for your hunt. If you're having a birthday party, the treasure hunt could be the last event, and the treasure could be each guest's party favor. Or, the last clue could lead to a box of candy bars for all the searchers to share. Your hunt will be more challenging if you divide the group into teams. Write several sets of clues, leading each team to its treasure.

Try this: Hold your treasure hunt outdoors, and use natural clues—like certain trees, rocks, or flowers.

Disappearing Man

If you've ever watched "Wheel of Fortune" you'll know this game. In this case, though, the game is played like Hangman, only in reverse.

A Spider's Web

Start your Halloween party off right with a spider-web treasure hunt. You'll need some yarn or twine—one length for each guest. Starting at a point far from your front door, tie your treasure to the yarn, stash it in a hiding spot, and begin to wind the yarn around various objects in the room. Move from room to room, zigzagging the yarn, until you reach the entrance to your home. Cut the yarn, and tag it with a guest's name. Do the same with each guest's yarn, crisscrossing it with all of the other strands. You'll end up with a big tangle of yarn, resembling a spider's web. As each guest arrives, hand her a web strand with her name on it. Your guests will have fun untangling themselves and rolling up their strands as they seek the treasure.

Each player is given paper and a pencil and told to draw a stick figure on the paper. The figure can have as many or as few features as the group decides, but all the figures must be alike. One person is chosen to be the leader. She thinks of a familiar phrase or rhyme and draws blank lines on a piece of paper, one blank for each letter. She leaves a space between blanks to indicate a new word.

If the phrase is "better late than never," her paper looks like this:

— — — — — —   — — — —

— — — —   — — — — —

As she shows the group her paper she says, "My first word has six letters, my second word has four letters, my third word has four letters, and my fifth word has five letters."

Each girl draws the same blanks on her paper, under her stick figure.

Now the first girl might ask the leader, "Are there any Es?" The leader puts Es in the blanks where they belong and shows her paper to the group. Each girl then fills in her paper likewise. The game continues, with every player getting a turn to suggest a letter. If a player suggests a letter that isn't in the phrase, however, she must erase one section of her figure: a head, arm, leg, body, or neck.

The game is over when somebody guesses the phrase. If a player makes so many wrong guesses that her figure is completely erased, she must drop out from the game.

POOF!

Modern Manners

Introductions

There are only a few rules for this and they aren't very hard:

When introducing a kid to an older person, always mention the older person first.

Examples:

"Grandma, this is Hannah Sunshine. Hannah, this is my grandmother, Mrs. Traveller."

"Dad, this is Nick Johnson. Nick, this is my father, Mr. Strange."

Or, if your parents prefer to be called by their first names:

"This is my father, Howard."

You shouldn't call an adult by his or her first name unless you know it's okay with that person. Some grown-ups consider it really disrespectful.

When introducing a woman to a man, the woman's name should go first.

"Aunt Sue, this is my coach, Mr. Salineri. Coach, this is my aunt, Sue Smart."

When you are introduced, look at the person, smile, and say: "Nice to meet you." That's it. Unless you happen to think of something especially interesting, you don't have to say anything else.

The handshaking rule: Girls and women may or may not shake hands with each other. If a woman doesn't offer her hand to you, just smile and say, "Nice to meet you." Boys and men shake hands with a woman or girl only if she offers her hand first.

Special Situations

If you're introducing a woman to the President of the United States, the President's name goes first:

"Mr. President, this is my mother, Mrs. Strange."

If the President offers your mother his hand, she will, of course, shake it. She should wait for him to offer it, though.

Be sure to explain that to her if she should ever meet the president.

Royalty always goes first, too.

"Your Royal Highness, may I present my father, Mr. Strange?"

It's a one-way street with presidents and royalty. People are presented to *them*—never the other way around.

Thanks

When do you have to write a thank-you note? When a gift is given or sent to you and the person is not there to be thanked personally. Get your thank-you notes out fast, or they'll just hang over your head and the person who gave you the gift will have hurt feelings or be annoyed.

Your letter can be short, but try to make it friendly;

> Dear Aunt Martha,
> Thanks for the socks.
> Love,
> Joanne

This isn't good enough. Add something that shows you put a little effort into it:

"Thanks for the socks. I really, really needed them because all my old ones have holes in them. And blue is my favorite color, too. I'll think of you every time I put them on."

And if you hated the socks, don't let your Aunt Martha know!

Spanish: Poor *fahvor; Grahs*-yahs
French: Seel-voo-*pley;* Mare-*see*
German: *Bit*-teh; *Don*-keh-shern
Dutch: *al*-stu-bleef; *donk*-oo vell
Italian: per-fav-*oh*-ree; *grotz*-ee-ya
Hindi: Me-har-ba-ni seh; Shu-kri-ya
Swahili: Ta-fahd-*ha*-li; A-*sahn*-tay sana
Chinese: Ching; Sye-sye
Russian: Pah-*zhahl*-stah; Spahs-*see*-bah

Phone Manners

Decent phone manners are simply a combination of common sense and courtesy.

If you're making a call, always greet the person who answers the phone and always identify yourself.

"Hello, this is Jennifer. May I please speak to Amy?"

Barking, "Is Amy there?" into the phone might get the job done, but you sure won't get points for politeness.

And if you're the one answering the phone, you've got to be polite, too.

Caller: *"Hello, is your father there?"*

You: *"No, I'm sorry, he's not. May I take a message?"*

When you take a message, write it down, and always repeat it back to the person to make sure you've got the name and phone number right.

A Death

Even adults sometimes don't know quite what to do or say when someone dies. A kid whose best friend's father died unexpectedly had this good advice:

When my best friend's father died, my friend really didn't want to talk about it. All I could do was be with him as much as possible. I wanted him to know that I was always willing to talk, but I waited for him to bring the subject up. It took a long time. I used to think, "C'mon already—you should talk about it!" but he just wasn't ready.

Right after his father died, lots of kids called to say they were sorry. It was nice of them to call, but I could see it made him uncomfortable. Maybe it would have been easier if they had sent notes. I'm not sure.

My friend's father died a couple of years ago. Now sometimes I'll be the one to bring up his father. For example, "Did you do that with your Dad?" Right after his father died I waited for him to bring his father into the conversation.

I guess my best advice would be this: You should be ready to talk, but take your cues from the other person, especially right after the death.

Friends

Friendship's most basic rule should be pretty familiar: *Treat other people the way you want to be treated.* Be considerate of other people's feelings. Don't be a show-off, don't be mean or overly critical, don't lie, and if you do something wrong, learn to say "I'm sorry." If someone apologizes to you, accept the apology and try not to hold a grudge.

Here's what one girl had to say: "Always stick up for your friend. If she's done something wrong, tell her so in private, but not in front of other people."

Be a Good Sport

Take the good as well as the bad with a smile. Good sports-manship goes beyond games and into how you behave at school, at home, and with your friends.

It's not always easy to be a good sport, but try anyway. Don't sulk or whine if you lose. Don't make excuses like, "I hurt my leg" or, "The sun got in my eyes." Don't blame your teammates or taunt your opponents.

A good sport is also a good winner—don't gloat! And, of course, never cheat.

How to Be Unpopular

Follow this simple advice and you're guaranteed to lose old friends and make new enemies

■ Always make yourself the center of attention. Hog the spotlight and talk, talk, talk. If they aren't listening, just talk louder! *You're* the only one worth listening to, anyway.

■ Make sure everyone knows you're the most interesting girl around. If something exciting happened to someone else, be sure to tell people that the same thing happened to you, only better (or much, much worse). If Rachael says she's going to Disney World, tell her that's nothing: *You* got to go after closing time with a private party. (Your uncle has connections.)

■ Talk about your friends when they're not around. Don't say anything *too* bad—just let everyone know that Emily's dad went on the class trip because he lost his job. Or Megan's so very nice it kinda makes you wonder. All *you* need to do is plant the seed. With luck, others will get credit for the rumor.

■ Make plans with your friend and if something better comes up, break the date. (She doesn't mind—at least she's never said so.)

■ Make a habit of borrowing things from people—pencils, books, money, clothes, etc. Wait a few months before returning them—if you return them at all. *You'd* lend *your* stuff to them; they've just never asked.

■ Say whatever is on your mind, no matter how it makes people feel. You're just being honest, that's all. Besides, they shouldn't be so sensitive. If Mollie's new haircut makes her look like a cockatoo, be sure to tell her so!

■ Always demand to get your own way. If Sarah wants to play detective and you want to play horse, let the other girls know that Sarah's idea is stupid, and you won't have any part of it.

That's all it takes. Just follow these guidelines, and you'll soon get your number of friends down to the one or two who are too scared to tell you what they really think of you.

How to Make a Friend

Everyone feels a little shy when it comes to making new friends. There's always a chance that your show of friendship will be ignored or rejected. Sometimes, though, you just have to take a chance.

Look around you and see if there's a girl who seems like she'd be fun to know. See how she treats her other friends. If she treats them well then chances are, she'd be a good friend to you, too.

Introduce yourself and ask her questions about herself, her family, and what she likes to do. Really listen to what she has to say. Look for things you have in common.

If she doesn't respond, remember that some girls who seem stuck-up are really just shy. Give her the benefit of the doubt. If she really is stuck-up, forget her and find someone better.

How to Set the Table

The basic rule is knives and spoons on the right, forks on the left. The napkin can go on the plate, next to the fork, or under the fork. When you have more than one fork, you place them in order of use from left to right for each course. So if the salad is served first, then put the salad fork on the

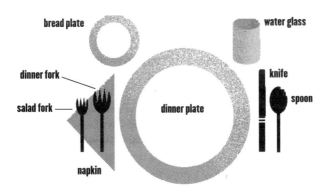

bread plate

water glass

dinner fork

knife

spoon

salad fork

dinner plate

napkin

left, outside of the other forks. If fish is served next, then put that fork next and so on. If you remember this rule, all the grown-ups at the table will watch you and follow your lead, because many of them have forgotten how to use fancy place settings.

If you're going to be *really* fancy and correct, bread plates go above the forks, and water glasses above the knife and spoons.

Setting the Table in the Middle Ages

Ever heard the phrase, "He's a real trencherman"? Back in the Middle Ages, instead of plates people ate from flat pieces of stale bread, called *trenchers*. The trenchers soaked up gravy, and any uneaten bit of plate, or trencher, was tossed to the dogs or given to the poor.

Forks were unknown in the Middle Ages. People carried around their personal spoons and knives, though. Two diners often shared a single trencher, bowl, or cup. Lots of people died from mysterious diseases.

Tipping

When you and your friends go to a restaurant, remember to save enough money for a tip when you're deciding what to order. A standard tip is about 15 percent of the bill. Don't be intimidated by the math! Here's a pretty easy way to rough out 15 percent:

■ First, figure out 10 percent, which is a snap: if your bill is $4.79, 10 percent is about 47 or 48 cents. Ten percent of $11.62 would be about $1.16. Once you have 10 percent, just divide that amount by 2 and you have 5 percent. Add the two numbers together and you've got your 15-percent tip. For example:

■ Your bill is $7.51. Ten percent is about 75 cents. Half of that is about 38 cents. Add those together to get $1.13 for a 15 percent tip. But it's easier to leave $1.15 so you don't have to count out pennies. Or $1.10. The tip doesn't have to be exactly 15 percent—just approximately that amount.

Of course, you can always use a calculator—but every girl should know how to figure 15 percent!

Taxi drivers and hair stylists expect to be tipped, too.

Where Did Tipping Come from, Anyway?

One theory goes that it started in the 1600s, when restaurants had boxes near their entrances with T.I.P. written on them. *T.I.P.* was short for "To Insure Promptness." Anyone who wanted to be served quickly would drop a few coins in the box before sitting down to eat.

How to Tell If a Boy Likes You

As you already know, boys are strange. What they say and do doesn't necessarily have anything to do with how they feel. If a boy likes a girl, he doesn't always show it by acting nicely. In fact, he doesn't usually show it, period. Here are some clues, though:

■ You know a boy likes you if he's even more annoying than usual.

■ You know a boy likes you if he acts differently around you than he does around his other friends, or other girls.

■ You know a boy likes you if he acts rougher around you than he does around other girls.

■ A boy who thinks he's cool will act like a jerk. A nice boy will act nicer.

■ You know a boy likes you if he throws an iceball at you after school. (Just don't let him get away with it.)

Vulgarity

Four-letter words and graphic dramatizations of certain unmentionable body functions are no substitute for cleverness or humor. You know that, but there are some kids—mostly boys—who haven't figured it out yet. Here's some advice from other girls who have been there, too.

Some things you can do the next time you witness vulgar behavior:

■ Just ignore them.

■ Walk away.

■ If they won't stop, warn them that you'll tell a teacher or parent.

■ Tell a teacher or parent.

Some things you can say:

■ "Excuse me, did I just hear a voice?"

■ "Where were you raised, in a barn?"

■ "You're linguistically inhibited. Look it up."

■ "Do you feel better now?"

■ Look at them, shake your head and mutter "Pathetic" as you walk away.

Advice
Some Good Advice

Always set goals. People who set goals for themselves get more done than people who don't. Make a list of what you want to do today. At the end of the day, check off the goals you've met. If you didn't get to something, put it on tomorrow's list. Most people worry about the things they *didn't* do, without appreciating what they've done. By the end of the week you'll see that you accomplished a lot more than you think you did! Set long-term goals, too. Don't worry about whether they're practical or not, it's better to aim high.

Be curious. When someone asked Albert Einstein how he thought up the theory of relativity, he answered, "I just never stopped asking 'Why?'" Ask "Why?" "How?" "If?" and "What?"—then set about finding some answers. You won't find the answer to every question, but you'll learn a lot more than the person who doesn't ask or who thinks it's too much trouble.

Be brave. Being brave doesn't always mean being a war hero or running into a burning building to rescue a toddler. You're brave if you stand up for something you know is right, even when no one else seems to agree with you. If you know something's unfair, speak out. People will respect you for it, and more important, you'll respect yourself.

Follow through. Everyone starts a project with lots of enthusiasm, and that's important. But the test comes when a project stops being fun and starts to be just plain work. If you make yourself follow through the first time, you'll find that each time after, it gets easier and easier.

More Good Advice

Have a sense of humor If you can laugh at yourself and your mistakes, you'll be more understanding of other people's mistakes. Use humor to try to keep your problems in perspective. Of course, there are some problems that are just too serious to laugh about, but most aren't.

Like yourself. There's a difference between laughing at yourself and putting yourself down. It makes people just as uncomfortable to hear you tearing yourself down as it does to hear you tearing down someone else. Take some time to appreciate the good things about yourself.

Be as honest as you can. Lies and half-truths have lives of their own. You may think you've gotten away with them, but they always return—and bring their friends! You should not only try be straight with others, but be straight with yourself, too. If more than one person has said the same thing about you—especially if it's something you'd rather not hear—you may need to listen. There might be some truth in it.

Be flexible. If history has taught us one thing, it's that nothing ever stays the same. Don't become so attached to an idea that you become stuck. Keep yourself open to new ideas and experiences. It's important to know your own mind and to stand up for what you think is right, but if someone has a different opinion, hear them out politely. Even if you disagree, try to remember that other people's ideas have value, too.

Even More Good Advice

Here's some advice the writer F. Scott Fitzgerald gave to his 11-year-old daughter, Scotty.

Things to worry about:
Worry about courage.
Worry about cleanliness.
Worry about efficiency.
Worry about horsemanship.

Things not to worry about:

Don't worry about popular opinion.

Don't worry about dolls.

Don't worry about the past.

Don't worry about the future.

Don't worry about growing up.

Don't worry about anybody getting ahead of you.

Don't worry about triumph.

Don't worry about failure unless it comes through your own fault.

Don't worry about mosquitoes.

Don't worry about flies.

Don't worry about insects in general.

Don't worry about parents.

Don't worry about boys.

Don't worry about disappointments.

Don't worry about pleasures.

Don't worry about satisfactions.

Things to think about:

What am I really aiming at?

How good am I really in comparison to my contemporaries in regard to: (a) Scholarship (b) Do I really understand about people and am I able to get along with them? (c) Am I trying to make my body a useful instrument or am I neglecting it?

Stuff to Put in Autograph Books and School Year Books

Remember, if you write it in ink, it's there forever—and that's how you'll be remembered!

YY U R   U R 2 good
YY U B   2 B 4 gotten
I C U R
YY 4 me

Remember Jack
Remember Jill
Remember the girl
Who writes downhill.
(write this line "downhill")

Remember the city
Remember the town
Remember the girl
Who ruined your book by writing upside down.
(write this upside down)

Remember the season
Remember the weather
Remember the girl
Whorunsallherwordstogether.

Remember the north
Remember the south
Remember me
And my big mouth.

Remember M
Remember E
Put them together
And remember me.

Be a smart girl
And live at your ease
Get a rich husband
And do as you please.

Yours 'til butter flies

Yours 'til lip sticks

Yours 'til France fries Turkey in Greece

Yours 'til the kitchen sinks

These are good for Valentines to boys, who think they are cute and clever:

Roses are red
Violets are blue,
I like pecans,
Nuts to you.

Roses are red
Violets are blue
Everybody stinks,
And so do you.

Roses are red,
Violets are blue,
Garbage is smelly,
And you stink, too.

Stuff to Put on Computer E-mail Messages

;-)	Wink
:'-(	Crying
:-*	Kiss
:-!	Smoking a cigar
":-"	Devil
:-)8	Man wearing bowtie
(:v	Duck
d:-)	Baseball player
*:o)	Clown
:-#	Braces
:-[	Vampire

3

Social Studies

Girls grow up eventually, and grown-ups have a big responsibility to make sure society functions smoothly and wisely. Here are some things to know about some major institutions.

How the Government Works

Checks and Balances

The Constitution distributes federal powers among three distinct branches of the government:

- The Legislative branch (Congress), which makes the laws
- The Executive branch (the President), which carries out the laws
- The Judicial branch (the Supreme Court), which interprets the laws

To make sure too much power isn't concentrated in any one part of the government, the writers of the Constitution divided the power so that each of the three branches acts as a check on the other two. For example, the President is Commander-in-Chief of our military, but only Congress can declare war.

This constitutional system of checks and balances was designed to keep a single person or a small group from seizing power.

How to Write to Your Representative and Senators

First, find out your Representative or Senator's name. If you aren't sure, look in a newspaper or ask your parents or teachers, or go to the library.

Address your envelope like this:

> Senator (senator's name)
> United States Senate
> Washington, DC 20510

> Representative (representative's name)
> United States House of Representatives
> Washington, DC 20510

In your letter, start off by using this fancy form of address at the top of the page:

> The Honorable (name)
> United States House of Representatives
> (or United States Senate)
> Dear Representative/Senator (name):

Then write your letter. Be sure to include your name and address after your signature so your legislator can respond to you.

Congressional Facts

House of Representatives

The term of office for Representatives is two years. (The entire House is elected every two years.) To qualify as a representative, you have to be twenty five years old, a US citizen for seven years, and you have to live in the state from which you're elected.

■ All revenue bills (having to do with taxes and spending) are introduced from the House.

■ The House has the power to *impeach,* or remove, civil officers.

- If no presidential candidate gets a majority of electoral votes, the House elects the President.
- The head of the House is called the *Speaker*.

Senate

Senators serve for six years. Like Representatives, they can be re-elected. To serve as a Senator you have to be at least 30 years old, a U.S. citizen for nine years, and live in the state where you're elected.

- The Senate confirms all appointments made by the President.
- It approves treaties and tries anyone who's impeached.
- The Vice President presides over the Senate.
- If no vice-presidential candidate gets a majority of electoral votes, the Senate elects the vice president.

Presidential Facts

The term of office for the President is four years. A President can be re-elected once. To qualify for President, you have to be thirty five years old, a native-born citizen, and a resident of the United States for fourteen years.

- The President is Commander-in-Chief of the armed forces.
- He negotiates treaties with foreign governments, appoints federal officials, can pardon any offense against the federal government except impeachment, and can *veto* (say "no" to) bills passed by Congress.

Impeachment

If the President or any other high government official breaks the law, the Constitution offers a way to help solve the problem:

Article II, Section 4 of the Constitution provides that the President can be removed from office by the process of impeachment if accused of treason, bribery, or other "high crimes and misdemeanors." The House has the power to impeach. If the President is impeached, the next step is a

The Order of Succession to the Presidency

These are the people, in order, who take over if the president dies or leaves office for some reason.

1. The Vice President
2. Speaker of the House
3. President *pro-tempore* of the Senate
4. Secretary of State
5. Secretary of the Treasury
6. Secretary of Defense
7. Attorney General
8. Postmaster General
9. Secretary of the Interior
10. Secretary of Agriculture
11. Secretary of Commerce
12. Secretary of Labor

trial before the Senate. When that happens, the Chief Justice of the Supreme Court acts as the presiding officer—not the Vice President. So far, no President has ever been removed from office by impeachment.

Facts About the Supreme Court

No qualifications for membership in the Supreme Court are stated in the Constitution. You don't even have to be a lawyer to be a Supreme Court Justice.

The Court consists of one Chief Justice and eight Associate Justices. Each member of the court is appointed by the President and must be approved by the Senate. Supreme Court appointments are for life, unless a Justice is impeached. But Justices can retire if they wish.

The Supreme Court hears cases in which a state or the federal government is involved; cases dealing with ambassadors or other foreign ministers; and cases appealed from lower courts, especially if there's a Constitutional question.

Democrats and Republicans

These two major US political parties can trace their roots back to the early days of our country.

Democratic Party

The Democratic party is the oldest political party in the country. It developed from the Anti-Federalist party led by Thomas Jefferson. This Anti-Federalist party first called itself the "Republicans." After the Federalist party died out, the Republicans were the only party, but they soon split into two wings, the Democratic Republicans and the National Republicans. Under the leadership of Andrew Jackson, the Democratic Republicans became known simply as "Democrats," the name they've kept ever since.

As a rule, Democrats look to government for help solving problems in society.

Republican Party

Although it didn't come into true existence until much later, the Republican party traces its origin back to Alexander Hamilton's Federalist party. When the Federalist party fizzled out, the opponents of the Democratic Republicans (Jefferson's party that went on to become the "Democrats") called themselves National Republicans.

This group went on to become the Whig party, which opposed Andrew Jackson's Democrats. In 1854, the Whig party splintered over the issue of slavery. Out of this division

The Flag

Each part of the American flag is symbolic. Traditionally, the red on the flag stands for courage, white for liberty, and blue for loyalty. The 13 stripes represent the 13 original colonies. Each star represents one state.

a new, third, party was formed: the Republicans. Abraham Lincoln was the first Republican President.

As a rule, Republicans look to individual to help solve problems in society.

There are many other, smaller parties in the US, including the Libertarian Party, the Green Party and the Reform Party.

The American Eagle

Benjamin Franklin wanted the wild turkey to be our national bird, but he didn't get his wish. Congress chose the American Bald Eagle as our national bird in 1782.

The eagle is now protected by law. It is illegal for anyone except for members of certain Indian tribes to have or collect eagle feathers. The name "bald eagle" comes from how the white feathers look on the bird's head—not because it's bald.

You can find the Bald Eagle on the National Seal, coins, military badges, and other government objects.

Families

The primary political unit in every society is the family. The more stable and secure families are, the better and healthier society is.

A Family Experiment

Every family has a set of rules—the way things work—even if its members don't know it. Try writing down the "rules" for your family and sharing them at the family table. You'll be surprised at how many family members you surprise!

Parents

Parents are human. They can't always keep their problems to themselves. Still, it's not fair for them to involve you in their fights and it's especially not fair for them to make you choose sides. If one (or both) of your parents is doing this, point out to them that their fighting upsets you. Suggest that they talk over their differences when you're not around, or that they take a nice long walk, to work things out. Point out that you love them both and you only like taking sides when watching your favorite team.

Too-strict parents. You might be surprised to learn that most kids would rather have parents that are a little too strict than not strict enough. When they make rules about your behavior—even if they seem overly strict—your parents are showing you they really care about the things you do—and who you do them with. Learning about life is a little like learning to fly an airplane. Once you get in the air it's exciting, but first you need to know which buttons to press and which ones to leave alone. If your flight instructor puts you in a plane and says, "Figure out the rules yourself. Good luck!" you know you're in trouble. It's the same with parents.

You Need to Earn Your Parents' Trust. If you can do this now when you're young, they'll trust you later with bigger things. In other words, if they can't count on you now to bring in your bike at night, you're going to have trouble getting the keys to the family car later on.

Siblings

It may be asking too much to be best friends with your brother or sister, but you can make things go smoother if you have a few ground rules. Here's how some girls have dealt with the fighting-between-siblings issue:

- Be the bigger of the two, and ignore what he or she just did or said. This is hard!
- Stop yourself before you hit or yell. Talk it out.

Kids on Allowances & Chores

"I get $2.00/wk, if I do chores. Chores: Have to make and pack my 6-year-old brother's lunch every day." **(age 10)**

"I get $10.00/wk. I get paid the same day every week. I'm expected to pay for candy, small things like beanie babies, fairs, and carnivals with my allowance. Chores: Fold the laundry and carry it upstairs; vacuum; clean my room every day; walk the dogs two times a day; set the table every night; go to the corner store for small things. If they ask me to do something, I do it—no questions asked!" **(age 10)**

"I don't know how much allowance I get. It's kind of casual. If I want something, they pay for it with my allowance. It's kind of an I.O.U. system. Chores: Walk and feed two dogs every day. Clear the table every night." **(age 11)**

"I get $1 or $2 for special things, like watching my 6-year old sister, when my mom goes to the gym. If I need something, they pay for it. If it's something big, or something they don't want to buy, it comes out of my birthday or Christmas money. I don't have to do any regular chores." **(age 11)**

■ Stop yourself before bringing your parents into it. Can it be worked out between the two of you? Chances are, your parents will still be looking for a solution long after you and your sibling have forgotten all about the problem.

■ If you must have it out, make some fair fighting rules, like:

1. No hitting (or kicking or spitting).

2. No yelling.

3. No name calling.

4. No accusing.

Relatives

Aunt: Your mother or father's sister, or their brother's wife.

Uncle: Your mother or father's brother, or their sister's husband.

Cousin: Your aunt and uncle's child.

First cousin, once removed: Your mother or father's cousin.

Second cousin: Your parent's cousin's child.

Great-aunt or great-uncle: Your grandparent's siblings. (Genealogists call this relationship grand-aunt or -uncle.) A great-aunt is (for instance) your grandmother's sister.

Half-sibling: Your mother or father's child with a previous spouse.

Step-sibling: Your mother's husband's (or father's wife's) child from a previous marriage.

Divorce

Whether it's your own parents who are divorcing, or a good friend's parents, this is never easy. Even knowing that lots of other kids—over half the marriages in this country end in divorce—are going through, or have gone through, the same thing doesn't make it easier.

If it's your parents who are breaking up, remember that your mother and father are divorcing each other—they're not divorcing you or your brothers and sisters. Try not to take sides, even if you're tempted. If your parents complain about each other to you, ask them not to. As a matter of fact, even if your parents aren't divorced, don't let them get away with this kind of thing—it puts a kid in a terrible position.

Sometimes it's very hard to tell your closest friends that your parents are breaking up. Try to do it, though, so you won't feel as though you're carrying a horrible secret around. It's almost always better to talk things out.

Occasionally you'll already know that a good friend's parents are separating, but your friend might be having a hard time telling you. If that happens, after a couple of weeks bring it up yourself, but in a natural, sympathetic way. You might say, for example, "I'm sorry about your parents." You don't have to say too much; just let your friend know you're aware of the situation, and that you're still her friend.

Religion

Here are the five largest religions in the world. We've listed them according to how long ago they were established.

Hinduism

This is the oldest of all the major religions and the largest religion in India. Hindus believe that after death they are reborn (reincarnated) into different bodies. They believe that if they live decent lives, their *karma* will be good and they will be reincarnated as prosperous or spiritual people. (On the other hand, if they are wicked, they might come back as beggars—or even animals.) Hindus worship many individual gods, like Siva, Ganesh, and Hanuman, but believe that all these gods are just different parts of the one great power—Brahman. To show their respect for the gods, Hindus bathe every day and offer the gods food and incense on small alters in their homes. The *Bhagavad-Gita* is a Hindu book of scripture.

Judaism

Jews believe that nearly 6,000 years ago, one god, Yahweh, revealed his laws to the people of Israel through a prophet named Moses. Before Judaism, the people of Israel had believed in many gods. The most sacred writings in Judaism are the Bible (what Christians refer to as the *Old Testament*) and the *Talmud*—commentaries on the *Bible* written by holy men called *rabbis*. The *Bible* contains a history of humankind and of the Jewish people—beginning with Abraham, who is considered to be the first Jew. It also contains God's revelations to the many Jewish prophets who followed Abraham. Each Jewish temple (called a *synagogue*) keeps a scroll (the *Torah*) with the Laws of God written on it. Jews believe that God will someday send a *messiah*—a holy messenger—to solve all the problems of the world. Jewish holidays include Passover (which celebrates the Jews' safe passage from Egypt and slavery) and Rosh Hashanah. Jewish children enjoy celebrating Hanukkah and Purim. When they are thirteen, Jewish boys and girls have a bar- or bat-mitzvah, respectively. For this coming-of-age ceremony, they must memorize and recite passages from the *Bible*.

Buddhism

Gautama Buddha was a wealthy prince who lived in Northern India over 2500 years ago. He gave up his position and riches in order to seek knowledge, called *enlightenment*. One day as he sat thinking under a banyan tree, he was suddenly filled with all the knowledge of the world. He understood that humankind could become free of the cycle of birth, death and rebirth only if we treated our enemies with kindness, and stopped looking for happiness in worldly things. Any person able to do this would achieve *nirvana*, or eternal happiness. Buddhists hope to attain enlightenment and reach nirvana by practicing a deep kind of thought—called meditation—and by following the example provided by Gautama, the Buddha. From India, Buddhism has spread to China, Tibet, Japan, and Southeast Asia.

Christianity

Two thousand years ago, a Jew named Jesus was born in Bethlehem, Israel. Before his birth, prophets had predicted the coming of a Jewish messenger from God. Some Jews believed that this baby was the Messiah, or Christ. As a young man, Jesus proclaimed himself to be the promised Messiah and began teaching throughout the land. He began to attract followers, and amazed them by performing miracles, such as healing the sick, walking on water, and bringing the dead back to life. Jesus explained that he would sacrifice his life on Earth so those who believed in him would have eternal life in heaven—and soon the rulers of the land decided that Jesus was a threat to their power and Jesus was put to death. Three days after his death, it was reported that Jesus' body had risen, resurrected from death, and later he was seen visiting some of his followers. In these visitations, Jesus promised eternal life to anyone who would follow his example. Like Buddha, Jesus Christ taught forgiveness and compassion. He urged people to put their faith in godly, rather than worldly, things. The Christian *Bible* is divided into two sections: the *Old Testament* and the *New Testament*, which records Jesus Christ's life and death. Major Christian holidays are Christmas—which celebrates Christ's birth—and Easter, the holiest day in the Christian calendar, which celebrates Jesus's resurrection.

Islam

Like Christianity, Islam also has its roots in Judaism. It is the most recent of all the major religions, and the fastest-growing. Muslims believe that the Messiah came to Earth 1,300 years ago and that his name is Mohammed. The prophet Mohammed showed people how God wished them to live and worship. God's word is written down in a holy book, called the *Koran*. All devout Muslims pray five times a day, no matter where they are. When they pray (on special rugs which they carry with them) they always face the holy city of Mecca, in Arabia. Once a year, all Muslims show their respect for God by fasting during the holiday called *Ramadan*. Ramadan lasts for one month, and during that time, Muslims are not allowed to eat or drink during daylight hours. Fasting reminds all Muslims that their bodies are less important than their souls, in the eyes of God. At the end of Ramadan, there is a great feast. All Muslims are expected to make a pilgrimage to Mecca at least once during their lifetimes.

All five of the world's major religions share a belief in one powerful God, rather than many deities. They all teach respect towards others, both in thought and deed. In all five religions, failure to obey religious laws has very serious consequences. For some, this means a cycle of birth and rebirth in a series of lifetimes, while for others the punishment is separation from God, in this life or after death.

what other kids like

We asked a lot of kids what kinds of books they liked and which movies they liked. We also asked parents what they thought. Here are some of our "poll" results:

A Random List of Things Kids Say Other Kids Should Know by the Time They're 12

- How to introduce themselves to strangers
- How to navigate their hometown, buy stuff at a store and return home
- Have a library card and know how to use the library
- How to say simple words in one foreign language
- How to order at a restaurant
- Basic mastery of geography: the four oceans, seven continents, etc.
- How to feed themselves (prepare a meal; make a snack)
- How to relate to the opposite sex in an appropriate way
- Basic telephone etiquette
- How to do homework without parental prodding or oversight

- Basic mastery of one musical instrument (drums not included)
- How to ride a bike
- How to swim
- Skill in at least one sport
- The approximate dates of:
    - The American Revolution
    - The Civil War
    - World War I
    - The Great Depression
    - World War II
    - The Civil Rights movement
- Basic things about the human reproductive system

Top Five Board Games:

- Risk
- Stratego
- Monopoly
- Clue
- Chess

Bonus: 13 Dead-End Drive

Top Five Card Games:

- Poker
- Casino
- Hearts
- Gin
- War

Favorite Movies

Most of these have stood the test of time!

- *Wizard of Oz*
- *Around the World in 80 Days*

- *Lady and the Tramp*
- *The Court Jester*
- *Hans Christian Andersen*
- *The Thief of Baghdad*
- *A Night at the Opera*
- *Seven Brides for Seven Brothers*
- *On the Town*
- *Damn Yankees*
- *Robin Hood* (the Errol Flynn version, of course!)
- *Fort Apache*
- *Casablanca*

Girls' Favorite Movies

- *The Swiss Family Robinson*
- *My Fair Lady*
- *The Three Ages:* Buster Keaton
- *The Paleface:* Buster Keaton
- *The Parent Trap*
- *Sons of the Desert:* Laurel and Hardy
- *That Darn Cat!*
- *Little Women*—either the version with Winona Ryder or the one with Katherine Hepburn.

Favorite Animated Movies

- *Lion King*
- *Sleeping Beauty*
- *Cinderella*
- *Snow White*
- *Jungle Book*
- *101 Dalmatians*
- *Lady and the Tramp*
- *The Aristocats*
- *The Little Mermaid*

A List of Great Books for Kids

If you haven't read the books on this list yet, you're in for a real treat!

- *The Wind in the Willows* by Kenneth Grahame
- *The Chronicles of Narnia* series by C.S. Lewis
- *Charlotte's Web* and *Stuart Little* by E.B. White
- *A Wrinkle in Time* by Madeleine L'Engle
- Anything that was written by Roald Dahl
- *The Oxford Book of Poetry for Children* compiled by Edward Blishen and illustrated by Brian Wildsmith
- *Bible* Stories
- *Stories for Children* by Isaac Bashevis Singer

Favorite Books for Girls

- *The Little House* series by Laura Ingalls Wilder
- *Emil and the Detectives* by Erich Kastner
- *A Cricket in Times Square* by George Selden
- *The Borrowers* by Mary North
- *The Twits* by Roald Dahl
- *Black Beauty* by Anna Sewell
- *Sarah, Plain and Tall* by Patricia MacLauchlin
- *Pollyanna* by Eleanor H. Porter
- *Misty of Chincoteague* by Marguerite Henry
- *Fifteen* by Beverly Cleary

A Reading Club Start a "literary society" in your neighborhood with other kids. This is a great way to share ideas about the things you've read—and find out about new books and authors you might like.

Here's how it works. Hold a meeting and elect a *convenor*. The convenor is the person who convenes the meetings of the society. At the first meeting, decide which book everyone should read. Then every week meet and discuss the book together as you read it. The whole club should focus on the same book at the same time and all club activities should be about the book.

For example, let's say you choose *Black Beauty* by Anna Sewell. One week, you might visit a stable to see the horses. Another week, you might draw pictures of horses. If the meeting is on a rainy day, you might hold it at the library and look at pictures of different kinds of saddles and horse breeds. Or you might check out a copy of the movie "Black Beauty." Once you're all done with *Black Beauty,* you can start on a new book—maybe *Misty of Chincoteague,* another great book about horses!

4

Safety, Hygiene & Grooming

Safety First

The first thing to do in an emergency is *remain calm*. Of course, it's easier to remain calm if you know what to do next. Here's some information we hope you'll never need.

Fire

- If you have a clear path, get out of the building right away and don't go back in for ANYTHING.

- Call the fire department from a neighbor's house.

- If you are on fire: STOP, DROP, and ROLL.

- If you're in a smoke-filled room, get down on the floor. Smoke rises. If you can, place a wet towel over your nose and breathe through it.

- If there's a fire in the next room and you have no way to get out safely, close all adjoining doors. NEVER OPEN THE DOORS if you suspect a fire in the next room. Touch the door carefully to see if it's warm. If it is, jam wet towels or pillow cases in the space between the door and the floor. Don't open any windows until the door is well sealed. (An open window can create a draft, attracting the fire.) If you can, turn on the shower and get in it.

- If you're in a tall building, tie something white to a stick and wave it out the window, so fire fighters can find you.

- If there isn't any water or a fire extinguisher around, you can put out a small fire with sand or dirt. (For example, grab a potted plant and dump the dirt on the flames.)

"Rotten Eggs"

Luckily, most people in life are good. But there are some "rotten eggs" out there. The problem is, you can't usually tell who's a rotten egg and who isn't. They don't wear signs. That's why it's important to trust your instincts and use some common sense. If a stranger (or even someone you know) is acting overly friendly or offering you stuff, be on your guard. (Be especially cautious if the person wants to take you somewhere where there aren't other people around.) It's not normal for a grownup to want to be your best friend. If someone's acting like they want to be a "special friend," let them know that you already have a best friend—someone your own age. If a stranger makes you feel uncomfortable, get away as quickly as possible. Never let strangers get you by yourself. Never speak to strangers in cars, no matter what.

Thunderstorms

In a thunderstorm, lightning is drawn to tall objects like trees and buildings. Though you'll want to find shelter under a tree, make sure it's not the tallest one around. Also, don't stand on a tree's roots or touch its trunk during a thunderstorm: when struck by lightning, the electrical charge runs through a tree—from the tips of each branch to the ends of each root. It will also travel through the ground surrounding the tree.

All tall buildings are equipped with lightning rods (a metal rod that runs from the roof to the ground, attracting and absorbing any electrical charge) so you're safe even in a very tall building. Golfers are sometimes hit by lightning because they stand out on the fairway. If you're on a beach or golf course (or any other flat, featureless area), lie down flat on the ground, until the storm passes. But stay away from the water. You're usually safe in your car, because the rubber in a car's tires doesn't conduct electricity.

Tick Removal

These three proven tick-removal methods work on both people and pets. Use them to remove regular ticks (not the tiny ones that carry Lyme disease. If you think you have one of these, call your vet or doctor for advice).

Method One: Cover the tick with petroleum jelly. Wait a few minutes for the tick to back out. Grab it and flush it down the toilet. If this doesn't work, try method two.

Method Two: Place several drops of turpentine or kerosene on the tick. When it backs out, remove and destroy. If neither of these methods work, you'll have to resort to method three (it's gross but it always works).

Method Three: Place the prongs of a pair of tweezers on either side of the tick's body. Carefully rotate the tweezers as you pull up (like unscrewing a bottle top). Gently pull until the whole tick pops out. Destroy. If you aren't careful, you may just remove the tick's body, while leaving the head embedded. If this happens, dab alcohol on the spot where the head is. Continue dabbing until the tick falls out.

It's not necessary to run to the doctor every time you get a tick bite, but make sure you always wash the bitten area thoroughly with soap and water after removing one.

Hair, Skin, & nails

Curls

Girls with straight hair have been curling it for centuries, while girls with curly hair have envied straight, smooth locks. In the 1960s, girls used to *iron* their curly hair to make it straight!

Hair should be damp (not wet) before curling. A spray bottle filled with water will keep your hair damp as you work. When setting your hair, start at the top-middle and work your way down, going from side to side.

Pin Curls: Take a small section of damp hair and, starting near the scalp, twist it around your index finger. Slide your finger out and flatten the curl against your scalp. Crisscross two bobby pins over the curl. Continue this way, until all your hair is pinned. Set your hair before bedtime and put a Lycra swimming cap over your head to keep your curls from coming out. Sleep on it (if you can!) and remove the pins in the morning.

A Hairdo Cover from an Old Pair of Tights

Leaving about 6 inches attached to the top, cut off the legs of an old pair of tights (Lycra tights work best) and discard the pieces. Now tie the legs together. You'll have a hairdo cover that doubles as an emergency swimming cap. If you fringe the ends of the knot, your cap will have a tassel!

You'll sleep a little better with:

Rag Curls: Cut or tear long strips from a piece of woven (not knit) fabric. Working from the top-middle, take a strip of fabric and tie it to a small section of damp hair. Leave about an inch of material on the tied end. Wind the hair around the rag. When you get to the end of your hair, tie the remaining rag to the extra piece, on top. Cover head with a setting cap and sleep on it. Carefully untie the rags in the morning.

Washboard Curls: Make lots and lots of little braids in your damp hair. Put small barrettes on each end (or dip your fingers in setting gel and "seal" the ends.) In the morning your hair will be frizzy—like a washboard!

Hair-Wrapping

Make a small, tight braid. Take three different-colored lengths of embroidery thread, each one twice as long as your hair. Tie the embroidery threads together at one end, then tie that end to the top of your braid. Pick one color and begin wrapping it very tightly around the braid and the other strands of thread. When the wrap is 1/2" long, pick a different color and put the thread you were just working together with the braid and the other two strands. Wrap that thread tightly for 1/2", then pick up the third color. Continue this way until you run out of hair (or thread). To tie your wrap off, cut one thread and wrap the last color around the braid and the other thread. At the end, tie the two threads together, then cut.

$1.00 sendaway for a Fancy Tail

For a neat tool to make fancy ponytails, send a dollar to Gift Club, Box 411-FT, Thiells, NY 10980. Include your name and address so they know where to send it.

Skin Deep

There's a saying that beauty is only skin deep. That's not true, of course, since many hearts are beautiful and so are all souls. But it is a good reminder to keep the part of us that everybody can see—our skin—nice and clean.

- Use gentle soaps and shampoos.
- Rinse well.
- Don't scrub! You'll tear your face off! (Well, you'll irritate it at any rate.)
- Pat your skin dry.
- Be careful of using water that's too hot. It's not good for your skin.
- Use a light moisturizer to keep your skin soft.

A Word about Make-up

The whole point of make-up is to make grown-up skin look as beautiful as young skin. So if you have young skin and you put make-up on it, you're sort of defeating the purpose. Also, *one sure sign of a kid*—too much make-up. Girls who don't have experience applying make-up almost always apply way too much of it because they think it will make them look older. It doesn't. It makes them look younger!

Give Yourself a Manicure

Step 1
- Remove the old polish.

Step 2
- Wash your hands really well with soap and water. If you have a nail brush, brush the tops and underneath the nails. The warm soapy water not only cleans your fingers and hands, but softens up the cuticles—those strips of hardened skin at the base and sides of each nail.

Step 3

■ Clip and file your nails. Nothing looks worse than one or two long nails sticking out from the pack. Cut all your nails to the length of your shortest nail (unless it's really short). With an emery board, file the corners so they are gently rounded.

Step 4

■ Push back the cuticles with a cuticle stick. If you care for your nails once a week, you'll be able to "train" your cuticles not to spread too far onto the nail.

Step 5

■ For a really professional look, put a base coat of clear polish on each nail before putting on a color. This strengthens the nail, and also helps the colored polish to go on smoothly. Put just enough polish on the applicator to do one nail without redipping. Use as few strokes as possible. Paint a stripe down the middle, then one on each side. Try not to touch the cuticle with your brush. Put base coat on all of your nails, then:

Step 6

■ Let the nails dry completely! Drying your nails between coats is the secret to a really professional-looking manicure. Don't use your hands until you're sure the nails are dry.

Step 7

■ Put on the top coat of polish. (Some manicurists put on three coats, but you don't need to go that far.) Apply it the same way you did the base coat. Because the tips tend to chip off, gently swipe the very tip of each nail with a tissue. Your nails will stay unchipped a little longer. Polished nails are fun, but know when to take the polish off; bare nails look much better than chipped and repainted nail tips!

Wardrobe

You don't have to have *everything* on this list, but here's a good idea of what many girls like to wear.

Fall (back-to-school)

■ 1 pair of sturdy school shoes or sneakers
■ Rain boots

- Party shoes (for fall/winter; black patent leather is, of course, seasonless)
- Hiking-boots or high-topped boots (optional)
- 1–2 skirts or
- 2 dresses (one a jumper)
- 1 pair of jeans
- 1 pair of sweatpants
- 1–2 sweatshirts (one zippered)
- 1 pair of overalls (optional)
- Several long-sleeved shirts
- 1 white blouse
- At least 7 pairs of underpants
- 3 camisoles (or singlets or bras)
- Red, black, blue, and white tights
- 1 pair of heavy cotton multi-colored tights (optional)
- 1–2 pairs of leggings
- Crew and knee socks
- Fall/winter party dress (optional)
- A dressy coat (optional)
- Cardigan sweater
- Polarfleece pullover or cardigan
- Backpack

Winter (in addition to fall)
- Snow boots
- Wool or heavy cotton pullover
- 1–2 turtlenecks
- Snow jacket and pants and/or a snowsuit
- More dark tights
- A holiday dress (optional)
- Outerwear: gloves, mittens, hats, ear-warmers, scarf

Spring
- Lightweight sneakers or slip-ons
- Spring/summer party shoes (if needed)
- Light-colored tights

- Light-colored jumper and matching shirt
- Several short-sleeved t-shirts
- White socks
- Short overalls (optional)
- Spring/summer party dress (optional)
- Fresh underwear

Summer (in addition to spring)

- Sandals
- Waterproof sandals, Jellies, or aqua shoes
- 2 swimsuits
- 2-3 pairs of shorts (1 pair mesh or Supplex)
- Several sleeveless T-shirts
- Sundress (optional)

5.

Stuff to Eat

O f all the things you can make, food is one of the things that's most fun for everybody.

Snacks

Cinnamon Toast

You will need:

- A medium-size jar with lid
- 1 cup sugar
- 2 tablespoons cinnamon
- 2 slices of bread (per person)
- Butter or margarine

Put the sugar and cinnamon into the jar, put on the lid and shake until mixed. Toast the bread. Spread butter on the toast and sprinkle a teaspoon of the cinnamon-sugar mixture on top of each slice.

Cinnamon . . .

C innamon comes from the inner bark of a tree that grows on the island of Sri Lanka (in the East Indies). It was one of the precious spices that Columbus was seeking when he accidentally bumped into North America.

Popovers

You will need:

- A muffin pan (the heavier the better)
- Butter for greasing muffin pan
- A flour sifter
- A hand mixer or whisk
- 1 1/2 cups of flour
- 1/2 teaspoon salt
- 3 eggs
- 1 1/2 cups milk
- 2 tablespoons melted butter

It's the steam inside them that makes popovers "pop." The secret is to have an oven that's not too hot (they'll brown before they pop) or too cold (they'll flop, not pop). So—after you've gotten all your ingredients together and greased your muffin tins, heat your oven to 450°, then:

Sift the flour and salt into a mixing bowl. In another bowl (or a large measuring cup) beat the eggs, milk, and melted butter together. Slowly, add the liquid to the dry ingredients, mixing with a hand-mixer or a whisk all the while. Continue mixing for two minutes, or until the batter has no lumps and is the consistency of melted ice cream. Pour the batter into the well-greased muffin pan. Fill tins up a little past halfway (the batter will rise a lot) and put the pan in the middle of the oven. Leave it there for fifteen minutes, then reduce the temperature to 350° and continue baking the popovers another 20 minutes. *Do not open the oven door,* or your popovers will be flopovers. Take them out and serve immediately. If you want to get fancy, mix together some softened, whipped butter with your favorite jam and spread in the steaming popovers. Makes 12.

Plain & Fancy Muffins

You will need:

- 2 cups of flour
- 3 teaspoons of baking powder
- $1/2$ teaspoon salt
- $1/4$ cup of sugar
- One egg, beaten
- $1/4$ cup of melted butter
- 1 cup of milk
- A flour sifter
- A muffin pan
- Cupcake liners

Set oven temperature to 400°. Sift your dry ingredients together into a mixing bowl. In another bowl or a large measuring cup, mix the egg, milk and melted butter together until well mixed. Next, add the liquid ingredients to the dry ones, and stir just enough to dampen the flour. *Do not overmix,* or the muffins will be tough. Fill the cupcake-lined muffin pan two-thirds full. Bake at 400° for 25 minutes. Makes 12 muffins.

Now that you know the basic muffin mix, you can experiment. Add bananas, nuts, raisins, berries, apple chunks, chocolate chips, M & M's, poppyseeds, lemon juice, dried fruit, cheese—anything you can think of. Just remember if you're adding a liquid ingredient, make sure you reduce the amount of milk so that your total liquid doesn't exceed one cup.

Tea Sandwiches

You will need:

- One loaf of white sandwich bread, minus "heels"
- One loaf of wheat sandwich bread, minus "heels"
- Circle, heart, or star-shaped cookie-cutters
- Fillings for the sandwiches, such as:
  - American cheese and baloney
  - Ham & Swiss cheese (with mayonnaise or butter, if you like)
  - Tuna or chicken salad
  - Peanut butter or cream cheese and jelly

Assemble the sandwiches by putting your favorite filling between one slice of white and one slice of wheat bread. Cut out a shape with a cookie-cutter and throw away the scraps. Place tea sandwiches on a platter and cover with plastic wrap right away (the edges will dry out and curl up, if you don't).

Why We Call It a Sandwich

Back in the eighteenth century an English lord—the Earl of Sandwich—was the first person to come up with the idea of putting meat between two pieces of bread, rather than eating each item separately. For his brilliant contribution, the resulting snack was dubbed a "sandwich." Sandwiches were often eaten at tea-time (4:00 in the afternoon) rather than for lunch, as they are today.

Real Food

Quesadillas

You will need:

- 2 flour tortillas
- A handful of grated Monterey Jack or cheddar cheese
- A pastry brush

In the microwave: Place the flour tortilla on a microwave-safe plate and put a handful of Jack or cheddar cheese in the middle of it. Brush water around the edges of the tortilla, and place another tortilla on top to make the quesadilla. Press down on the quesadilla, flattening the cheese and pressing out any trapped air. The water will "glue" the two tortillas together. Cover the quesadilla with a damp paper towel, and nuke for one minute.

Remove from oven and cut into wedges, like a pizza. Serves 2.

Some variations for the adventurous: Add refried beans, shredded, cooked chicken or beef, sweet or mild chile peppers, olives, etc.

The Origin of "Jack" Cheese

The Jacks were a large land-owning family in the town of Monterey, California. They produced a mild, white cheese at their ranch, which came to be known as "Jack's cheese."

Weineritos

Weineritos can be microwaved or steamed, but we don't recommend cooking them in a conventional oven, because the tortillas will dry out.

For each person, you will need:

- One corn tortilla
- One hot dog
- Catsup
- One slice of American cheese

In the microwave: Soften the tortilla first, by putting it on a microwave-safe plate with a dampened paper towel on top. Cook for 30 seconds. Take the tortilla out of the oven. Put on the tortilla: a piece of American cheese, a hot dog, and a little catsup. Now roll up the tortilla and put it, seam side down, on the plate. Cover with the paper towel and "nuke" for an additional 45 seconds. If you are cooking more than one at a time, weineritos should cook for one minute.

A Brief History of the Hot Dog

It all started with the Babylonians, who came up with the idea over 3,000 years ago of stuffing meat into animal intestines—the first sausages. The Greeks and Romans loved sausages, too.

A German city, Frankfurt, had its own version of the sausage, which became known as the "frankfurter."

Another nickname for frankfurters was "dachshund" sausages— named for the little, long German dogs they resemble. The story goes that in 1906 a cartoonist named Tad Dorgan was watching a baseball game and heard a vendor shouting, "Get your red hot Dachshund dogs!" He thought a picture of a real dachshund in a bun, covered with mustard, would make a good cartoon. He sketched it, but wasn't sure how to spell "dachshund," so settled for "hot dog." The rest is history.

Plain Cheese Pizza

You will need:

- One package of fast-rising dry yeast
- $2\frac{1}{2}$ cups of flour
- 2 teaspoons of salt
- A spoonful of sugar
- 1 cup of hot tap water
- 1 small can of tomato paste
- 8 ounces of shredded mozzarella cheese
- Some vegetable oil (olive is best)

The crust First, wash your hands. Put the entire package of yeast and a spoonful of sugar in a large mixing bowl. Add one cup of hot-but-not-scalding water and stir just enough to mix the yeast evenly in the water. When the mixture begins to bubble (this is the live yeast, growing) add one cup of the flour and stir with a sturdy spoon. Gradually, add one more cup of the flour, until the mixture is too thick to stir.

Pour a little oil onto your hands and rub them together. Gently begin to punch the dough in the bowl, first with one fist, and then with the other. When the dough begins to stick to your hands, add the remaining $\frac{1}{2}$ cup of flour a little at a time. When the pizza dough feels springy under your hands—usually after 5 minutes of kneading—cover the bowl with a damp towel. Put the bowl in a warm place for about 45 minutes, or until the dough is twice its original size.

While the dough is rising, preheat the oven to $500°$ and oil a round pizza pan or a cookie sheet. This is a good time to grate the cheese, if you didn't buy it pre-shredded.

Check to see if the dough has finished rising by poking your finger into the middle of it. If the dent stays, it's time to take the pizza dough out of the bowl (it will collapse a little) and put it in the pan. Gently push and stretch the dough until it covers the pan. Fold over the outside edges of the dough to make a raised crust.

The topping Scoop out some tomato paste with a spoon or your fingers and spread it on the dough. Spread right up to the edges. You don't need much—just enough for a thin, red layer. If you put on too much sauce, or it's too watery, the bottom of the crust won't cook through. Sprinkle the grated cheese evenly over the pizza.

Put the pizza on the lowest rack of your oven, and turn the oven down to 450°. After ten minutes, check to see how your pizza is doing. If the cheese is melted-but-not-burned and the crust is a golden brown, it's ready. If not, leave it in for another five minutes.

Really Fast Pizza

You can buy frozen or refrigerated dough at the supermarket. Or, you can substitute:

- A loaf of French bread, sliced lengthwise
- English muffin halves
- Flour tortillas or pita bread halves, for a really thin crust
- Biscuit dough

Prepare as for the Plain Cheese Pizza, above.

A Complete Stick-to-Your-Ribs Supper: Meatloaf & Mashed Potatoes

You will need:

- 2 lbs of ground meat: beef, pork, veal, turkey, chicken (or any combination)
- $^3/_4$ cup of bread crumbs
- 1 egg
- $^1/_2$ cup chopped onion

- Catsup
- 4 large Idaho potatoes
- 4 ounces (half a stick) of butter
- 1 cup milk
- Salt & pepper
- A loaf or deep-sided baking pan
- A mixing bowl
- A potato masher or sturdy fork

Before you start:

- Wash your hands!
- Heat oven to 400°
- Take out the butter and milk and let sit until it's time to mash the potatoes.

In a large mixing bowl, combine meat, bread crumbs, egg, onion, salt, and pepper. Using your hands, mix the ingredients together, until the egg and bread crumbs are evenly distributed in the meat. Put the meatloaf in a bread pan or mound it into a baking dish with high sides. Spread a layer of catsup on top and place the meatloaf in the middle of your oven.

Wash the potatoes. Prick a few holes in them with a fork and put them in the oven with the meatloaf. Cook the meat and potatoes for 50 minutes, then check the potatoes by sticking a fork in them. If it slides in easily, they're done. Turn the oven off and take out the potatoes, leaving the meatloaf in the oven.

Cut the potatoes in half, lengthwise. Place a potato half—flat side down—on a dinner plate, and pinch the skin together. The jacket will slide off, leaving the insides exposed. (Do this carefully, they're HOT!) Pick out any dark bits and put the potatoes in a bowl. Continue, until all of the skins have been removed. (If you *like* potato skins, put the jackets back in the oven, and let them crisp.) Add the milk, butter, salt and pepper to the potatoes and mash them with a fork or a potato masher.

Take out the meatloaf and drain off any extra fat. Move to a serving plate and slice. Serve with the mashed potatoes and a vegetable. Serves 4.

Treats

Pink Snowballs

You will need:

- 1 quart of strawberry or vanilla ice cream
- $^1/_2$ package of shredded coconut
- Red food coloring
- An ice cream scoop
- A cookie sheet

Scoop out the vanilla ice cream and place the scoops on a cookie sheet, one inch apart. Leave the ice cream out while you prepare the "snow." Place the shredded coconut in a mixing bowl and add one or two drops (no more!) of red food coloring. Stir until all the coconut is pink, then sprinkle it generously on the ice cream balls. The coconut should stick to the softened ice cream. Place the cookie sheet in the freezer and chill until the ice cream is hardened. Makes 6 to 8 snowballs.

Cake Basics

Its good for every kid to know how to make a cake from scratch. It's a little more work than a mix, but you'll taste the difference. Before you get started, though, there are a few things you need to know.

Flouring the Pan: Coat the bottom and sides of your pan with butter or margarine (not oil). Spoon some flour into the pan and tilt it from side to side until all the butter is covered with flour. If there are any uncoated spots, grease and flour again. If you don't, the cake will stick to these spots.

Cool Before Decorating: After the cake has finished baking, let it stand in the pan to cool for at least ten minutes. Place a wire rack over the top of the cake and turn both the rack and the cake upside down. If your pans were floured first, they should slide off the cake easily. Leave cake on the rack to cool *completely* before frosting.

Putting the Layers Together: When you put the two layers together, make sure the cake *tops* meet in the middle. First, put the flat (bottom) side of one cake on a plate; this will give you a nice level base for your cake. Frost the top generously, then place the second layer *top side down* on the bottom layer. Fill any gaps between the layers with frosting.

Icing the Cake: There's a trick to icing a cake. If you remember this order, you'll do fine: *Ice the sides, then ice the top.*

As you ice the sides, work from bottom to top, spreading the frosting with long, even strokes. Build up the top edges so they are a little higher than the cake's top. Next, heap icing

FYI

1 quart = 4 cups
1 pint = 2 cups
1 cup = 8 fluid ounces
1 cup = 16 tablespoons
1/3 cup = 5 tablespoons plus 1 teaspoon
1 fluid ounce = 2 tablespoons
3 teaspoons = 1 tablespoon

on top of the cake, and spread it out from the center of the cake to the built-up edges. If you want a super-smooth surface, dip your spatula in warm water and smooth the icing on the cake's top. Dip your spatula again and smooth the sides.

Now you're ready to bake. Here's a basic layer-cake recipe.

You'll need:

- 1 cup of sugar
- $1/2$ cup (one stick) of softened butter or margarine
- 2 eggs
- $3/4$ cup of milk
- 2 cups of flour
- 3 teaspoons of baking powder
- 1 teaspoon of vanilla
- 2 round cake pans
- Butter and flour for flouring pans
- A flour sifter

Pre-heat oven to 350°. Cream butter and sugar together in a large bowl. Crack the eggs into a smaller bowl and beat for a minute, then add the milk. Stir milk and eggs together, then add to the other ingredients and mix.

Measure the flour and baking soda into a flour sifter and gradually sift them into the large bowl, stirring occasionally. Add vanilla. Beat by hand or with a mixer for two minutes. Pour into two floured cake pans. Bake for 45 minutes, then check for "doneness" by inserting a sharp knife into the middle of the cake. If it comes out clean, the cake is done. If some of the mix sticks to the knife, continue cooking the cake and check every five minutes, until knife comes out clean. While the cake is cooling, make some buttercream frosting. You'll find the recipe on the back of any box of powdered sugar.

Gateau

Modern recipes are a piece of cake ("gateau" in French) compared to the cuisine of pre-revolutionary France.

Marie Antoinette's Cake with Beau Icing

Cream together for exactly half an hour: 1 cup of butter and 1 cup of granulated sugar. One at a time, add 4 egg yolks. Very slowly, add one cup of milk. Add 1 teaspoon of almond extract. Sift 2 and 1/2 cups of flour 6 times, then add to the liquid mixture. Whisk egg whites until stiff (about ten minutes) and fold them into the cake batter. (There was no such thing as baking soda in Marie Antoinette's day. The whipped egg-whites helped make the cake rise.) Pour the batter into a tin cake pan and bake in a "slow" oven for 60 minutes.

Beau Icing: To 1/2 cup of hot water add enough powdered sugar to make a stiff, spreadable icing. Flavor

Homemade Peanut Butter

You will need:

- 3 cups (or a 16-ounce can) of roasted and salted cocktail peanuts

- 3 tablespoons of softened corn-oil margarine or butter

- A food processor or a blender

For creamy peanut butter: Place the entire contents of the can of peanuts into the bowl of the food processor and blend until they are ground to a paste and have begun to form a ball. Turn off the processor and add the butter. Resume blending, until creamy.

For crunchy peanut butter: Prepare as above, but add only 2 cups of peanuts, setting one cup aside. Blend until creamy, then add the reserved peanuts. Then blend or pulse for an additional 5 seconds.

Homemade Butter

One girl tells us, "We did this in our class. Everybody got a chance to shake the jar, and when we finished, we put the butter on some bread."

You will need:

- 1-or 2-pint container of heavy (whipping) cream
- Salt, to taste (optional)
- A large, mayonnaise-type jar with lid
- An old bandanna, or handkerchief-size square of cheesecloth

Pour the cream in the clean jar and close the lid tightly. Shake the jar until the cream separates into butter and buttermilk. Pour the contents of the jar into the cloth and squeeze out the liquid by twisting the cloth around the knob of butter. Run cold tap water over the butter to harden it, then press out remaining liquid from the butter. Scoop it out of the cloth and into a storage container.

Homemade Fudgesicles

You will need:

- A box of chocolate pudding mix (the kind you need to cook)

- 3 cups of milk

- A box of instant whipped topping (should be near puddings in the store)

- A large mixing bowl (for topping)

- A whisk or blender

- Popsicle sticks

- Popsicle molds or Dixie cups

- Aluminum foil

Following the directions on the box, cook one package of chocolate pudding. While the pudding cools, prepare the whipped topping, following the directions on its box. When the pudding is cool, add it to the whipped topping and blend for one minute.

Pour the mixture into the molds or Dixie cups. (If you're using Dixie cups, cover them with a small square of foil and insert Popsicle stick through a slit in the middle.) Freeze until firm.

Chocolate-Covered Frozen Bananas

You will need:

- 6 bananas
- A small (6-ounce) bag of chocolate chips
- Popsicle sticks
- A small cookie sheet
- A spatula

Peel the bananas, then cut them in half crosswise. Place a Popsicle stick in the end of each half. Lay the bananas on a cookie sheet and freeze them for several hours, until they are frozen solid. Melt the chocolate chips in a microwave or double boiler. With the spatula, spread melted chocolate on the frozen bananas. The chocolate should harden instantly. Wrap any uneaten bananas in aluminum foil and store them in the freezer.

Frozen Grapes

These are delicious on a hot summer day. Just place washed, seedless grapes in the freezer for a few hours.

Smoothie

If you use frozen strawberries, your smoothie will be nice and cold.

You will need:

- 1 banana
- 1 cup of fresh or frozen strawberries
- $1/2$ cup of milk
- $1/2$ cup of plain yogurt
- A blender or food processor

Put ingredients in a blender or food processor and blend until smooth. Makes 2 drinks.

Banana/Strawberry/Kiwi Drink

You will need:

- 1 banana
- 1 cup of fresh or frozen strawberries
- 1 kiwi, peeled
- 1 cup of orange juice
- A blender or food processor

Blend until smooth. Makes 2 drinks.

Black Cow

Put a scoop of vanilla ice cream in a tall glass. Pour root beer over the ice cream, until it fizzes to the top of the glass.

Milk Shake

For a Chocolate Shake: Put one or two scoops of softened vanilla ice cream in a tall glass. Pour some chocolate syrup on the ice cream, then add a little milk. Stir with an electric hand mixer or with a fork, breaking up the ice cream as you do. Continue stirring, until it's completely mixed.

For a Vanilla Shake: Instead of chocolate syrup, use a teaspoon of vanilla.

Make-Your-Own Sundaes

You will need:

- A few quarts of assorted ice cream (figure on one quart for every four people)
- Chocolate syrup
- Butterscotch sauce
- Assorted chopped nuts
- Crushed pineapple
- Maraschino cherries
- Bananas, sliced
- Several cans of whipped cream
- Chocolate and rainbow sprinkles

Arrange sauces and garnishes around the tubs of ice cream. Provide ice cream scoops and dishes. And don't forget the napkins!

6.

Fixing & Making Things

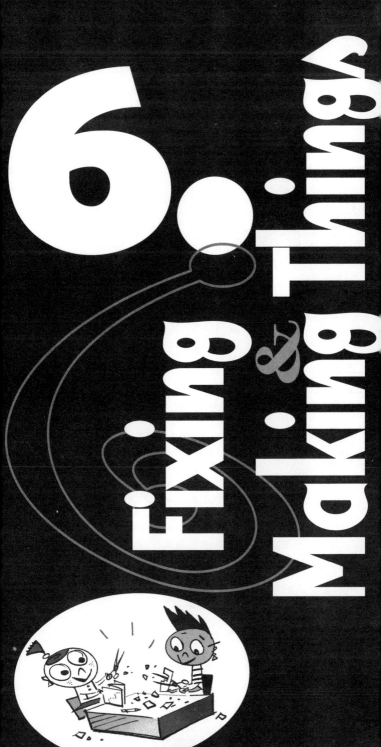

*S*ometimes, things fall apart, sometimes they break, and sometimes you just have to make something from scratch. Every girl should know how to make her world a better place, from the ground up.

Miss Fixit!

A Basic Carpenter's Kit

A carpenter is never far from her tool kit. Here's what they carry (and you should, too).

- **Box** or bag to keep tools in.

- **Hammer** Like baseball bats and bowling balls, hammers come in different weights. Try a few out, and choose one that's not too heavy. A claw hammer (one with a two-pronged nail-removing "claw") is more practical than a ball-peen hammer (a rounded counterweight on the other side of the business end.)

- **Nails** There are basically two basic kinds of nails—nails with flattened heads and nails without heads, or "finishing" nails. Nails are sold by length and weight. The higher the number, the longer (and thicker) the nail will be. Always keep an assortment of nails in your kit.

- **Phillips-Head Screwdriver** A screwdriver with a cross on the tip. Phillips-head screws are usually convex (curve out) rather than flat. This and the cross-shape make it easier for the screwdriver to grip the screw. Get a medium size screwdriver, with some screws to match.

■ **Slotted-Tip Screwdriver** This is a screwdriver that fits into the slots of flat-headed screws. Phillips-head screws are better for most jobs but you'll need this, too. Get a medium-size screwdriver.

■ **Hacksaw** This is a good basic saw for most small carpentry jobs.

■ **Pliers** The most commonly used are slip-joint pliers. These pliers have square, toothed grippers and can be adjusted for wide or narrow jobs. Also, many come with wire-cutters attached.

■ **Clamp** The most useful kind of clamp is a C-clamp (so called because it's shaped like the letter). Clamps are mainly used for holding two pieces of wood together after gluing. A 3-inch, light-duty C-clamp should do it.

■ **Measuring Tape** Get a retractable, steel measuring tape rather than the folding wood kind. Ten feet is enough for most jobs. You'll be tempted, but try not to play with it too much—it can break.

■ **Combination Square** This handy tool has more than one use: it's good for measuring and marking lines as well as right angles. Also, it has a level—which comes in mighty handy when you're trying to decide where to hang that shelf.

■ **Sandpaper** Get a combination pack with coarse, medium, and fine.

The Carpenter's Creed

Measure twice, cut once. If you follow it, you'll save yourself a lot of time—and wood.

Emergency Bike Repairs

How to Change a Flat Tire on Your Bike

Two pieces of gear any regular bike rider should own:

■ A patch kit, which costs $3 or less, and contains rubber cement, small pieces of sand paper, and patches—usually 10 or so

■ Tire levers, which are sold in groups of three, and also cost about $3 for a set

Here's What to Do:

■ Move far off the road to repair the flat.

■ Remove the wheel from the bike.

■ Make sure all the air is out of the tire.

■ Locate the side of the tire that's opposite from the valve. That's where you'll be working.

■ Putting your first tire lever on one side of the tire, pry gently. Be as careful as possible to avoid pinching the inner tube. Take the second tire lever and repeat the procedure about three inches away—on the same side of the tire. Keep repeating until one side of the tire is outside the rim.

■ Pull the stem of the inner tube out of the rim. Remove the inner tube from the wheel. Leave the tire half on/off the rim.

■ Very carefully run your finger along the inside of the tire to find and remove any sharp objects that might've caused the puncture.

Patching the Inner Tube

■ Blow the inner tube back up. Listen carefully to hear air hissing out of the leak area. If you can't hear anything, dip the inflated inner tube into water, a section at a time, and look for air bubbles: that will be your leak area. Be sure to dry the inner tube thoroughly.

■ Once you find the hole use sand paper to scrape all around the puncture area—clear about a one-inch radius.

■ Apply rubber cement to the area. Let it dry for about a minute.

■ Put the patch over the hole, making sure all sides of the patch are down smoothly. Press tightly against the patch area for a good minute.

■ Wait another three minutes.

■ Put enough air in the inner tube to make it firm—don't over-inflate.

Final Steps

■ Stick the stem of the valve back into hole in the wheel rim.

■ Put the tube back into the tire. Make sure tube isn't bunched up.

■ Using the tire levers, tuck the tire back into the rim. Be extra careful not to pinch the inner tube.

■ From a height of about two inches, bounce the tire all around to make sure it settles.

■ Reattach wheel.

Putting a Bicycle Chain Back On

There's no way to avoid getting your hands dirty with this job!

If you have a ten-speed, put the chain on the smaller ring. If you don't have a ten-speed, lift up the back tire and move the pedals forward half a rotation to get them out of the way while you work.

Replace the Chain in This Order

■ Thread the chain through hub in the back.

■ If you have one, thread the chain through the derailleur.

■ Bring the chain to the top of the front pedal sprocket.

■ Rotate the pedals slowly and the chain will fall into place on the sprockets.

Fixing a Leaky Faucet

Most faucet leaks are caused by bad washers. If you want to impress your dad, your mom, and yourself, fix it yourself! Let your parents know what you want to do, then:

■ Turn off the water, either in the main valve or at the valve under the sink, so you won't get a gushing flood when you remove the faucet. This is a really important step. Don't skip it.

■ Use a monkey wrench to unscrew the nut cap at the top of the faucet. Put a piece of cloth between the jaws of the wrench to keep from scratching the metal faucet.

■ Pull or twist out the spindle.

Faucet
Screw

■ Loosen the screw that holds the old washer in place and remove the washer.

■ Put in a new washer and replace the screw.

■ Replace the spindle and tighten the cap of the faucet.

■ After the faucet's tightened, turn the water on again at the valve.

Painting a Wall

The paint can will have directions—follow them!

Some painting basics:

■ Take off the old paint by scraping or with paint remover.

■ Fill any cracks or holes with spackle. Spread it on with a spackle or putty knife. Let it dry completely. Sand the spackled part with fine sandpaper.

■ Be careful not to overload your brush with too much paint each time you dip.

■ Paint *with* the grain of the wood using straight, even strokes.

■ Be sure the first coat is completely dry before you put on a second one.

Around-the-House How-To's

Damage Control

Here's how to remove some of the worst kid-stains:

■ **Magic marker out of upholstery:** Follow the directions on Capture spot remover or put some rubbing alcohol on a rag and blot the marks. Gently rub the area, until the color comes off on the rag. Keep moving to new sections of the rag, so you don't rub the color back into the fabric.

■ **Craft glue out of carpeting:** If the glue has completely hardened, you'll need to carefully cut it out with a small pair of scissors. If the glue is still soft, dampen a sponge and press it on the glue spot. Leave the sponge on the area for a while, then rub away the softened glue with a paper towel. Repeat until all the glue has been removed.

■ **Silly Putty out of upholstery:** With a knife, scrape off the excess Silly Putty. Spray WD-40 on the area and let it sit for a few moments. Scrape again with the knife. Continue spraying and scraping, until the Silly Putty is gone.

■ **Grass:** Rubbing alcohol will take away the grass stain, but it may take away the color on the fabric, too. Test it first, on a hidden area of the material. After letting the alcohol soak in, flush it off with cold running water.

■ **Greasy stains (chocolate, pudding, gravy, etc.):** Lay the fabric—stain side down—on a folded paper towel and pour some cleaning solvent through the fabric, onto the towel. Change the towel often. Rub pre-soak stick on stained area and launder.

■ **Blood stains out of fabric:** Dissolve one teaspoon of white vinegar in two cups of warm water. Pour the solution on the stain, just before laundering. If the bloodstain is on white fabric, dissolve a spoonful of bleach or peroxide in a cup of water, and pour it on the area. Rinse it in hot water, after a few moments. You can also try commercial pre-soak products, like Shout!.

■ **Pen-marks out of fabric:** Different pen manufacturers use different inks, so you'll need to try a few different things here. First, run cold—then hot—tap water over the spot. If that doesn't work let the fabric dry, then try rubbing alcohol. Pour a small amount of alcohol on the mark and let it soak in. Rub the area with an old toothbrush. If that doesn't work, try acetone nail polish remover. (First, check to make sure the acetone doesn't affect the color of the fabric.) If it's a ballpoint pen ink stain, you can also try spraying some hairspray on it, and then rubbing it gently with a paper towel. Finally, there are several commercial spot removers on the market, like Energine, Capture, and Renuzit, to name a few. Good luck!

To receive a free stain removal booklet, call 1-800-Crayola or write: Consumer Services, Binney & Smith Inc., P.O. Box 431, Easton, PA 18044-0431

The U.S. Department of Agriculture publishes a free booklet titled "Removing Stains from Fabrics." Write to them at: U.S. Dept. of Agriculture, Washington, DC 20250.

How to Make a Bed

You'll need a fitted sheet, a flat sheet, and pillowcases.

- Strip the bed and take off the old pillowcases. Put the old sheets in one of the pillowcases.

- Put the pillows in fresh pillowcases.

- Place the fitted sheet on the mattress.

- Lay the flat sheet on top of the fitted sheet with its deep-hemmed end up and its "right" side facing down. The top of the sheet's hem should be level with the head of the bed.

- Tuck the foot of the sheet under the mattress. (If using blankets, lay them on the top sheet, about a foot down from the head of the bed. Tuck in the foot of the blanket and sheet together, as described.)

- Fold down the top of the sheet so the deep hem is now facing right-side up.

- Tuck in sheet (together with blankets) on each side.

- Place a comforter or bedspread over the sheets and arrange the pillows on top.

A Makeshift Fitted Sheet

Place a flat sheet evenly on the mattress. Make a knot a few inches down from one corner and hook that corner over one corner of the mattress. Do the same with the other three corners.

A Basic Sewing Kit

It's important to keep all of your sewing stuff together, so you'll know where everything is if you need to make a quick repair.

Find a special box with a lid (a round metal tin, or deep cigar box, for instance) or buy a sewing box at a variety store. If you're making your own box, line it with felt. Here are some of the basic tools you'll need for your sewing kit:

■ Fabric (not paper) scissors

■ Spools of black and white thread, plus any other colors you may need

■ A 60" plastic measuring tape

■ An assortment pack of needles

■ A needle threader

■ A thimble or square of rawhide, for pushing needles through heavy material

■ A box of straight pins

■ A seam ripper

■ A pin-cushion

■ Tailor's marking chalk

■ Assorted buttons

■ Other important-but-not-essential items for your kit include: small scissors, elastic, Velcro, iron-on tape, bias tape, and nylon thread.

Tip: Always keep black and white threaded needles handy for quick jobs.

How to Thread a Needle

Your thread should be about as long as your arm. If it's too long, it will tangle easily. Cut the thread on a slant (so it's less likely to ravel) then give the cut end a quick lick. Glide the slightly-damp thread through the eye of the needle. Make a small knot at the very end of the thread.

How to Sew on a Button

Step 1

■ Thread the needle and remember to knot the end of the thread.

Step 2

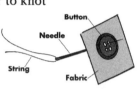

■ Pierce the fabric from the underside and come up through one of the button's holes.

Step 3

■ Go from that spot over the top of the button and come back down through any other hole; repeat until you've gone through each hole several times and the button seems securely fastened.

Step 4

■ Finish up on the underside of the fabric by knotting and then snipping the ends of the thread.

Start a Button Collection

You can usually find jars of old buttons at yard and rummage sales. Pick them up when you can, and be on the lookout for antique buttons. Mount your button collection by sewing them onto felt or velvet. You can display your buttons by color, size, or pattern —any way you like. Some button collections are worth thousands of dollars. In New York City a store called Tender Buttons sells nothing but old buttons!

Knitting Basics

When you knit, you're pulling yarn through a series of loops in order to make a solid piece of fabric. To get started, you'll need a pair of knitting needles and some yarn. Both needles and yarn come in different thicknesses: the thicker the needle, the bigger your stitches will be. If you're using big needles, you'll need thick yarn. (The beginner should use a size 10 needle and 4-ply yarn.)

To get the feel of it, start out by make a knitting sample: a square piece, 12 stitches wide by 12 rows long.

The first thing you'll need to do is to "cast on" a row of stitches. Here's how to do it:

Casting On

Step 1

■ Make a slip knot (a) and slide your needle through it (b). This is your first stitch.

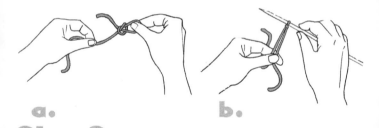

a.

b.

Step 2

■ Hold the needle in your writing hand and hold the yarn over your left thumb (c). (These instructions are for right-handed people; if you're left-handed, substitute "left" for "right".)

c.

Step 3

■ Pass the point of your needle under the yarn (d) and use your needle to make another slip knot (e). This is your second stitch. Repeat steps 2 and 3 until you have 12 stitches on your right needle. Transfer the needle to your left hand and pick up the other needle with your right hand.

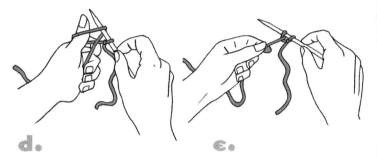

d.   **e.**

The First Row

Step 1

■ Put the right needle under and through the stitch closest to the point of your left needle (f).

f.

Step 2

■ Holding the yarn with your right hand, bring it under (g) and around (h) the right needle.

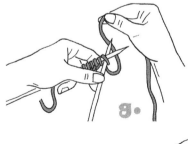

g.

h.

Step 3

■ With the right needle and the yarn in your right hand, pull the yarn through the loop on your left needle (i).

Step 4

■ Now, slide the stitch you have just made off the left needle and onto your right needle (j).

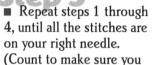

Step 5

■ Repeat steps 1 through 4, until all the stitches are on your right needle. (Count to make sure you have 12 stitches—it's easy to "drop" a stitch.) Take the needle with the stitches on it, and shift it to your left hand. With your right needle empty, begin to knit the second row. Continue knitting the rows back and forth, until you have knit 12 rows. Check your work: if your stitches were even, you should have a square. If not, it means that some of your stitches were tighter than others. In this case, unravel your sample and try again.

Step 6

■ After you've made a neat square, you'll need to bind the ends of your work, so it doesn't unravel. This is called "casting off."

Casting Off

Begin as if you were starting a new row. After two stitches, pass the first stitch over the second, then slide the first stitch over and off the needle. You should now have one stitch (the second) on your right needle. Knit another stitch, then repeat. Continue, until you have only one stitch left on your right needle. Cut the yarn and pull the end of it through the loop of your last stitch. With a needle and thread, sew the stitch in place.

Knit a Coathanger Cover

Use 2-ply (3/4 oz.) wool and size 4 needles. Cast on enough stitches to cover the length of a wooden coathanger (14 should do it) and knit enough rows to cover its width. Cast off. Sew down any loose ends. Slip the wool through the metal hook of the hanger, making sure that it's centered. By hand, sew the edges and ends of the wool together.

Embroidery

When you embroider, you're making special stitches with a special cotton thread on a plain cloth background. The special thread is called embroidery floss, and it comes in many colors. You also need a special needle for embroidery: one with an eye big enough for the floss to pass through. Though not essential, it helps to use an embroidery hoop. This is an adjustable frame that keeps the area you're embroidering stretched-out and easy to work. You'll find embroidery supplies at most department and craft stores.

Here are some basic embroidery stitches:

Running Stitch: Using an unknotted length of thread, bring the needle up from under the material you're working (A). Make a stitch (B), then pass the needle under and up at (C). Your visible stitch should be a quarter-inch long, while the space between stitches should be an eighth-inch long.

Back Stitch: Make a quarter-inch stitch *under* the material you're embroidering on. Bring needle up at (A), then backtrack and insert it into the hole you already made (B). Make a half-inch stitch under your cloth, and bring needle up at (C). Backstitch to (A), and continue going two stitches forward, one stitch back.

From a distance your stitch will look like one continuous line. This is an excellent stitch for outlining a design.

Rope Stitch: This is another good stitch for outlining a design. Working diagonally from left to right, bring the needle up at (C), which is (A) in the previous picture. With the needle pointing away from you, slip it back in at (D) and up again at (E). E has now become (C) for your next stitch. Repeat for the length of your outline.

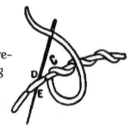

Cross Stitch: In the olden days, girls made samplers with cross stitch. You'll need an embroidery hoop for this stitch. It also helps to make very faint guidelines on your background material. You can buy premarked cross stitch patterns at craft or needlework stores.

Working diagonally, bring your needle up at (A) and put it back down at (B). Bring your needle back to (C) and re-insert it at (D). Work across from left to right. When you get to the end of the line, start to make your crosses. Working diagonally bring your needle up at (E) and insert it at (F). Work the line from right to left, until all your lines are crossed.

One fun way to learn embroidery while making a nice present for your mom or grandmother is to use a plain, white cotton hankie. Draw a picture on it, then embroider the picture. Be sure to draw the picture with something you can wash out later.

Note: Never use a knot when you embroider. To start, make a few running stitches along the line you're embroidering. End your work by weaving your needle back through several stitches, underneath the work.

Two Weaving Projects

To weave, you pass a single thread over and under a row of threads (called the *warp*) to make a solid piece of fabric. The cross-threads that are woven into the warp are called the *weft*. A *loom* is the machine that separates all the warp threads and makes it easier for the weft and warp to be woven together. The kind of loom that's used to weave most fabrics is a very large and complicated affair. You don't need one of these to try your hand at weaving. In fact, you don't need a loom at all. Here are two weaving projects that you can do without a loom.

A Grass Mat: This is a good outdoor weaving project, especially if you like pretending you're an Indian or pioneer girl. You can make some mats for your teepee or cabin—or a rug for your doll's house. Take four long, thin twigs or sturdy grass straws and cross them so their spokes are evenly spaced, as shown here.

The spokes will be your warp. Now, take a long strand of grass or straw and—starting in the center where the spokes cross—begin to weave it under and over the eight spokes. This will begin to look like a spiral. The grass is your weft. Continue weaving around the spokes, separating them as you do, until you come to the end of your grass. Take another strand and go back over the last few spokes you've already woven. Continue weaving this way—picking up a new strand where the old one leaves off—until you run out of warp. Slide the weft to the center of the circle and push the ends of your warp into it.

A Paper Placemat: Fold a large rectangle of construction paper in half, lengthwise. With scissors, cut crossways from the fold to a point one inch from the edge of the paper (a). Take a different-colored sheet of construction paper and cut it lengthwise into 1-inch strips. Weave the strips under and over the warp (b). Tack them at the ends with glue. To protect your placemat, lay it carefully on a sheet of clear contact paper, then cover it with another sheet. If you can get hold of a laminating machine (most schools have one) you can laminate your placemat—it'll last for years!

Try This: Instead of cutting a straight warp, make the cuts wiggly and wavy. Weave in string, ribbon, or raffia, as well as your strips of paper. You'll end up with a wild design! Seal or laminate.

For Loop Looms

If you have a loop loom, you can make your own loops by cutting the legs of old tights into 1/2" strips. Socks work, too.

Arts & Crafts

Wooden Bookends

Here's an easy woodworking project. You'll need:

- A piece of solid pine (ask for a one-by-four, two feet long)

- A saw

- A measuring tape

- A hammer

- Several 1" finishing nails

- Wood glue

- Fine sandpaper

When you buy the wood, ask the lumberyard to cut your 1 x 4 board into four 4" pieces. Or do it yourself: measure 4" from the end of the wood. Make three more marks, one mark every 4". To make sure your marks are square, use an index card. Saw into four pieces.

Work on a large piece of scrap wood or cardboard. Take one of the wood squares and hammer two nails into one side, $1/4$" from the edge. When the nails have just broken through the opposite side, stop. Turn the wood so the nail points are facing up. Spread some glue on the edge of another wood square and carefully position it on the two

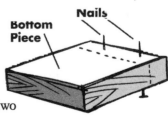

Nails

Bottom Piece

nail points. Gently tap the two pieces of wood together until the nails are all the way in. Do the same with the other two wood squares.

Gently Tap Nails in From Top

Side Piece

When the glue is dry, sand the bookends until smooth. If you wish, paint your bookends. To dress them up, glue an old wooden toy in the inside corner of each bookend (or cut an old wooden toy in half, and put one half inch each bookend).

White Glue

Front Half

Back Half

Three Picture Frames You Can Make

Take a special photo and make a frame for it.

Popsicle Stick Frame

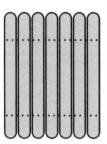

Cut down a 3" x 5" index card to make it 3" x 3". Glue 8 Popsicle sticks to the card (a). Lay a Popsicle stick crossways on each end on top of the row of sticks (b). Cut down a photograph, to make it 3" x 3".

b.

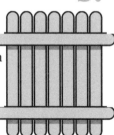

a.

Glue the picture on the frame (c). Lay two more sticks on each side of the picture, lengthwise (d). For a shiny finish, paint the frame with clear nail polish.

c.   d.

To make a stand for your frame, cut a 4" x 2" strip from another index card. Position it so the bottom of the strip is even with the bottom of the frame. Glue the top third of the strip to the back of the picture frame. Bend, and the picture will stand up.

A Shell Frame

Buy a small, pre-cut picture mat from an art supply or photo shop. Select a picture to fit in the opening of the mat. Glue the picture to an index card (or any card stock). Glue small shells, seaglass, coral and any other small beachy stuff around the frame. Let it dry. Glue the card stock to the mat, so that the picture is centered. Make a stand, as described above.

A Fabric Picture Frame

Cover the face of a pre-cut picture mat with a thin layer of tacky glue. Cut a square of fabric one inch larger than the mat on all four sides and lay it on the glue. Smooth, and pull it tight. Let the glue dry. With a single edge razor or an exacto knife, cut an X from corner to corner, in the frame's opening (see next page). Glue the triangles of cloth to the back of the frame. Cut out a square on each corner and glue the fabric to the

Mat

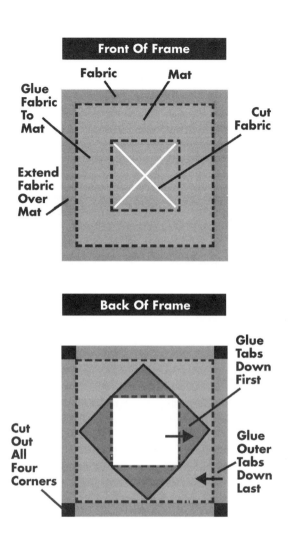

back. Glue a photograph to card stock so it's centered, and glue the card to the back of the frame. Make a stand, as described previously.

A Porcupine Pencil Holder

These are fun to make and they're good for giving as gifts, or selling. You'll need Sculpy, or any air-drying clay, and a pencil.

Shape a handful of brown clay into a large egg. Flatten it on the bottom. Pull one end of the egg out to make a long, pointed head. Put two small, round ears near the top of the head. Use a pencil to poke in two eyes. Roll a small clay ball and put it on the pointed end of the head for a nose. Make holes for the porcupine's quills by poking pencil holes into its back. To look like a real porcupine, the holes should be on a slight angle, away from the porcupine's head. Wiggle the pencil around in each hole, because the clay will shrink a little as it dries.

If you're using Sculpy or Fimo, put the porcupine on a cookie sheet and cook it at a very low temperature for an hour. If you're using regular clay, let it dry for a couple of days. Sharpen a box of pencils, and put them in the holes.

Make a Quill Pen from a Feather

The only tool you'll need is a penknife, or an X-acto-type knife.

Make sure your feather is big enough. In the old days, goose and turkey feathers were most commonly used.

■ **Clean the feather**. If you've found a fresh feather, scald the tip in boiling water for a couple of minutes. You want to make sure the end is clean so the ink will flow freely. The Dutch used to put feather tips in hot sand (140 in the oven) for a few minutes.

■ **Let the feather dry** overnight before you cut it.

■ **You have to clean off the cuticle** at the end of the shaft. The cuticle is the clear, smooth, hard, and shiny part. Use your thumbnail or a dull kitchen knife to peel away the cuticle.

■ **On the backside** of the feather you'll see a long dent. Using your thumbnail or a dull blade, scrape the pith (soft, squishy stuff) off the dent.

■ **Cut the tapered tip** of the quill off. Scrape out any *pith* you find inside the quill.

■ **Using your x-acto** or penknife, cut a scooped-out area on end of the quill. It should be about one-half inch from the tip.

■ **Now, cut a slit down the middle** of the feather tip. Make the cut as straight as you can.

■ **Very gradually shave** or cut the quill tip on each side until it forms a V at the center slit.

■ **Use an emery board** to smooth any rough spots.

■ **Soak your pen in water** for about 15 minutes before you use it—every time. This will keep the nib (or tip) flexible and less likely to break. Dip your pen into the ink and write or paint away!

Homemade Pomegranate Ink

To make your own pomegranate ink, you will need:

■ A pomegranate

■ Some cheesecloth or a loosely-woven material

■ A bowl

■ Gloves

■ A container for storing the ink

Remove the seeds from a pomegranate. Put them in a square piece of cheesecloth, twist the cloth, and hold it tightly shut with one hand. With the other hand squeeze the seeds until the juice runs through the cloth into a bowl. When you've collected all the juice you can, store it in a container. You might want to use gloves, because the juice stains—that's why it makes a good ink! Pomegranate ink looks red, but dries to a reddish-brown color.

It's a Drink, It's an Ink

American colonists made a red ink from the strained juice of boiled cranberries.

Apple Pomander

These are easy to make and they last for years:

You will need:

- An apple

- A bottle of whole cloves

- A 42" length of ribbon

- A paper bag containing cinnamon, nutmeg, and powdered cloves

First, wrap a Band-Aid around the thumb of your writing hand to protect it when you push the cloves through your apple. Pick up a clove and push the pointed end through the apple. Because the apple will shrink some, leave a little space between the cloves. Continue until your apple is completely covered with cloves.

Put the apple in the bag of spices and let it roll around. Take the apple out and shake off any extra spices.

Tie the ribbon twice around the apple so that your bow will be at the top—like wrapping a present. Make a double knot, then a bow. Tie the two loops of the bow together. There should be enough extra ribbon to hang the pomander.

Try This

Instead of an apple, use different-sized citrus fruits. Limes, oranges, and small grapefruits. (Lemons don't make good pomanders because their skin is too thick.) Proceed as in the activity, only make "pilot" holes first with a small nail to help push in the cloves. Roll the finished pomanders in the spices and put them together in a bowl. These pomanders don't need ribbons.

Pressed Flower Stationery

Pick delicate greenery and flowers and press them between the pages of a thick book. First, sandwich the plant material between two pieces of blotting paper. (Coffee filters make the best blotters, but you can also use tissue paper or newsprint.) The blotting paper absorbs any moisture in the plant, and lets it dry out faster. It also protects the pages of your book! After placing the flowers in the pressing book, stack other books on top of it for additional weight. Most flowers and leaves dry out in a week or two, but the thicker the plant, the more time it'll take to dry.

Some ideal plants for pressing are ferns, grasses, clover, honesty, Queen Anne's lace, hydrangea sprigs, pansies, buttercups, small daisies, sweet pea, and rose petals. Stay away from leaves or flowers that are fleshy or have bulky centers; they contain too much moisture and can't be pressed flat. (An exception is the thick-leafed plant known as lamb's tongue; it dries nicely and retains its velvety texture when pressed.)

To make pressed-flower stationery, take a sheet of good quality paper and spread a very thin layer of mucilage or library paste on top, in the middle of the sheet. With tweezers, pick up the pressed flowers and leaves and carefully place them on the glue. (Think ahead about how you want to arrange them, because once they're on the glue, they can't be moved again.) Let the glue dry before using.

Note: If you want your stationery to fit into a hand-made envelope, you'll need to cut the stationery in half, width-wise. This will leave you with two sheets of paper, each $8^1/2$ inches long by $5^1/2$ inches wide.

Making Envelopes for Your Stationery.

You can make an envelope out of one sheet of $8^1/2$" by 11" paper. First, make the rectangle into a square (try to do this without folding your paper.) Take your sheet of $8^1/2$" x $5^1/2$" paper and fold it in half. Using the diagram for a guide, place the stationery diagonally on the square of paper and trace it lightly with a pencil. Make notches, as shown in the diagram. Cut the tip off the first corner. Fold (1) to center. Fold (2) and (3) to center and glue in place. After putting your letter in the envelope, glue (4) down, or seal with sealing wax.

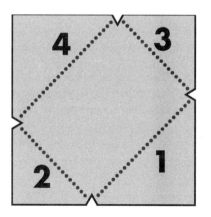

Flowers were once used as secret messages, conveying people's deepest feelings. If you were feeling angry and ill-used, you would send a bouquet of petunias and nettles to the offender. He might then send you a posy of peonies, signifying his remorse. Upon your next meeting, a sprig of mistletoe on the lapel would indicate your willingness to work through your problems. True love (forget-me-knots, roses) might lead to marriage (ivy) and eternal devotion (heliotrope).

Sugar Modeling (Alfinique)

In Mexico, November 2 is celebrated as the Day of the Dead (*El Dia del Muerte*). Like All Hallow's Eve (known as Halloween), this day is dedicated to the spirits of those who have died during the year. Relatives of the departed offer their spirits sugary skulls and skeletons decorated in pastel colors, called alfinique. You can make alfinique, too. Here's how:

Very slowly, add some water to several cups of granulated sugar. Stop when the mixture is just wet enough to hold together in a thick paste. With your hands, model the paste into a skull shape—or something more cheerful, like a bunny. Let the sculpture dry overnight.

Sugar paint: Put $1/2$ cup of powdered sugar into a bowl. (If you want to paint with more than one color, make a bowl for each color.) Add just enough water to make a smooth, creamy paste. Add a few drops of food coloring and mix well. Dip a paintbrush into the sugar paint and decorate your sculpture.

Mexican Cocoa

Add 1 teaspoon of unsweetened cocoa to 3 tablespoons of granulated sugar. Add 1/2 teaspoon of cinnamon, and mix. Pour a cup of hot milk into the cocoa mix and stir.

A Tissue Bouquet

You'll need colored tissue paper and four lengths of green florist's wire.

Step 1

■ Layer several sheets of colored tissue paper on top of each other and cut the stack into quarters. The layers can all be the same color, or each layer can be a different color.

Step 2

■ Take one tissue stack and begin to fold it back and forth, accordian-style, like you would a fan.

Step 3

■ When you have a long, skinny strip, round or fringe the ends of the paper (these will be the edges of the "petals").

Step 4

■ Fold the strip in half and wrap the wire two times around at the middle crease.

Step 5

■ Starting at the inside, begin to pull each layer of tissue paper up. Your flower will puff out.

Make three other flowers with the rest of the tissue paper. Put your bouquet in a vase and use it for a centerpiece—or give it to someone special.

A Real Grass Easter Basket

Cut a large sponge to fit in the bottom of an Easter basket. Three weeks before Easter, sprinkle some pre-soaked wheat kernels on the dampened sponge. Place the basket on a tray or plate. Add water each day, and spray with an atomizer. Your wheatgrass will begin to sprout in a day or two. In three weeks, your Easter basket will be filled with thick green grass! After Easter, give your grass to a needy cat.

Egg Coloring

Here are two different ways to color hard-boiled eggs. Remember, if you're dyeing an egg more than one color, always go from a lighter color to a darker one .

Coloring with Crayon The hard-boiled egg should still be slightly warm. Using only one color, draw a design on the egg. Take a tissue and rub off any extra wax. Put on a second color. Rub off. Continue with your design, putting on one color at a time. It's easy to make a rainbow using crayons. Put a stripe of yellow in the middle and layer stripes of green, blue, and violet going in one direction; orange, red and purple in the other.

Dyeing Eggs with Natural Colors

Use saffron or turmeric for yellow, beet juice for pink, red cabbage for violet, and boiled onion skins for golden brown.

Put the word "egg" in front of every vowel in a word.

"Degg-ooh yegg-ooh wegg-ant tegg-ooh gegg-o tegg-ooh thegg-a megg-all?"

"Negg-o. Legg-ets gegg-o tegg-ooh megg-eye hegg-ous egg-instegg-ed"

Translation: "Do you want to go to the mall?" "No. Let's go to my house, instead."

Tissue Egg Decoration

Take a strip of colored tissue paper and fold it, accordion-style. Cut out a design no longer than the length of an egg. The best egg designs are thicker in the middle

than on the ends. Spread a thin layer of mucilage-type glue onto a hard-boiled egg. Wrap the tissue around the egg, as pictured. Tear off extra tissue where the two ends meet. Carefully, smooth down the tissue, taking care not to tear it as you do.

A Secret-Message Valentine

■ Cut a large heart from a sheet of red construction paper.

■ At the widest part of the heart, lightly draw two parallel lines. With a single-edged razor or an X-acto knife, make a series of vertical slits every half inch between the lines.

■ Now cut a strip of white paper narrow enough to be threaded through the slits.

■ Next, decide what your message will be. If it is "I Love You," thread the paper between two slits and write "I" on the exposed white paper. Skip a few spaces and then thread it again, this time exposing enough paper to write "Love." Skip another few spaces, then thread the paper again and write "You." Make sure that you leave room between the words of your message. Now, pull the left-hand end of the strip of paper, so that your message can't be seen. On the blank white spaces, write the person's name. (You can also do it the other way—Have your message show, then when the tab is pulled, the name appears.)

■ Glue a tiny heart on the right-hand end of the strip and write "push" on it. Cut off any extra paper on the other end of the strip. Decorate the front of the heart with lace and seals and have Cupid deliver your valentine.

Some Old-Fashioned Valentine Messages

Of all that is near, thou art the nearest;
Of all that is dear, thou art the dearest.

Summer may change to winter, flowers may wither and die;
But I shall ever love thee, while I can heave a sigh.

A feast of flowers here behold, a thing of joy to see;
But ah! to me is sweeter still, to feast my eyes on thee.

Take this as love's sign;
And be faithfully mine.

A garland for thy hair I send;
For thou hath been a faithful friend.

Jewelry & Stuff

Three Braided Bracelets

Make some bracelets or anklets with colorful embroidery thread. String in beads and charms, and tie them onto your wrist or ankle. Wear them 'til they fall off! Make an identical bracelet for your best friend.

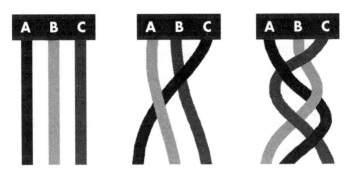

A Simple Braid Take three lengths of embroidery floss in three different colors. Tie them together on one end and tape that end to a table or the side of your shoe. Bring the right hand strand over the center, then the left-hand strand over the center. Tighten as you go. Add a bead from time to time to dress up your braid.

A Four-Stranded Braid Take four lengths of different-colored embroidery floss. Tie and tape. Bring strand 4 *under* strands 3 and 2, then *over* strand 1 only. Next, bring strand 1 *under* strands 2 and 3, then *over* strand 4. Continue braiding this way, working from one side to the other, then back again. If you get confused along the way just remember that the strand you're working is always the highest outside one. You'll probably need to practice this one a little before you start on a project.

A Rope Braid You'll need a pair of heavy, tightly-closing shears (for weight) and another pair of scissors, for cutting the thread.

To make a bracelet or anklet, measure one yard (36") each of two different colors of embroidery floss. Tie the two strands together at one end then thread them through the smaller hole on your heavy shears. Pinch the two ends (four strands) of floss together with one hand and let the shears dangle. (If the blades fall open, wrap a rubber band around them.) With your free hand, start to spin the shears around, so the two strands of floss become twisted together. When the floss is tightly wound, lay the shears down on a table.

Pinch the center of the bracelet with one hand, while you bring the two ends together with the other. Let go of the center fold: the floss will twist around itself, into a rope. Cut the floss from the shears with scissors and tie the ends of the bracelet together. To make a necklace, you'll need at least two yards of floss of each color. To make a thicker rope, use three strands.

Chain-Link Bracelet

Here's a piece of jewelry you can make that is kind of hard at first, but gets easier as you go—plus, you get to chew a lot of gum while you work.

To get started, you'll have to collect lots of gum wrappers. The long, skinny inside wrapper from a stick of gum is exactly the right size for a chain-link bracelet. (If you use the outside wrappers, your links will be too short . Save them for your bead necklace.)

Step 1
■ Fold the gum wrapper in half, lengthwise (a).

a.

Step 2
■ Unfold, and bring both edges to the center (b).

b.

Step 3
■ Fold together lengthwise, with the edges inside (c).

c.

Step 4
■ Fold in the center, crosswise (d).

d.

Step 5
■ Fold both ends to the center (e).

e.

Step 6
■ Fold in the center, crosswise (f).

f.

■ Repeat steps 1 to 6 with all your wrappers. To make a chain, link your wrappers together as follows.

Each link has two "arms." One side of each arm is folded and the other side is leafed. It's easier to work with the folded side when connecting your links. You will be slipping the arms of each link into the folded slots of the link before it. When you put the first two links together, your chain will have an L shape. The third link should go in the opposite direction and the fourth link will make your chain look like a W. Continue putting links into your chain until your chain is long enough to go around your wrist. Slip the last link into the slots of the first link and tape it in place with clear tape.

Bead Necklace

You will need:

■ 20 (or more) gum wrappers

■ Mucillage-type glue

■ Toothpicks

■ Scissors

■ Elastic cord

Cut triangular strips. Long strips will make small, thick beads and wide strips make wider beads. You can also make cylindrical beads by rolling up long narrow rectangles.

Place the strip color-side-down, and spread a thin layer of glue on the pointed half of the triangle. Place a toothpick on the wide end and begin to roll the paper up around the toothpick. Pull the toothpick out before the glue begins to set, and let your bead dry. (The mucilage will give your beads a shiny finish.) When you've made all your beads, string them on the elastic cord and tie it. For variety, string different-sized beads next to each other or string glass beads between each paper one.

Matching Earrings Tie a knot on one end of a piece of fishing line or nylon thread. String on a glass bead, then a paper bead, then another glass one. Make a knot on the thread, and tie it to an earring post.

Candy-Wrapper Jewels

Gum wrappers work best for this jewelry, but any paper will do. The individual links (or beads) look best when they're all made from the same kind of wrapper—especially when it's an easy-to-recognize brand.

Hardware Jewelry

A hardware store's a great place to find the makings for off-beat jewelry. It's filled with all kinds of chains and other neat stuff. With a little money and a lot of imagination, you can go into the jewelry business. Here are a few ideas:

Butterfly Pin

You'll need:

- An embossed ornamental brass cabinet hinge

- Superglue

- Rhinestones

- A pin-back. (You'll find these at craft or hobby shops.)

- Florist's wire or a strand of color-coded telephone cable wire.

- Put the hinge on a piece of cardboard or some newspapers, so you won't get glue on the table. Put superglue in the middle of the hinge and lift the two "wings" of your butterfly. Hold in position until the glue has set. Glue the rhinestones into the screw holes.

Brass Hinge

Coiled Wire

Rhinestones

■ Bend your wire in half and coil the tips, for antennae. Glue to the underside of the pin. Glue your pin-back to the back of the butterfly.

More Ideas

■ A ball-link chain (the kind of pull-chain you see on ceiling lights) makes a great necklace or bracelet for hanging charms. You'll have to go to a lighting store to get one. For hanging important stuff on your backpack, pick up a round-eye swivel bolt snap and sew it on. Be on the lookout for washers, coils, hex and wing nuts, and other small "charms."

■ Don't limit yourself to the hardware store, though. Check out stationery stores, sporting goods stores (for fishing tackle and weights) and other stores that sell specialized hardware. If there's a watch repair shop in your town, ask for any extra watch parts. Tiny gears and watch faces are perfect for making pins, earrings, and charms for a bracelet or necklace.

Jewelry Findings Catalog

Call the Jewelcraft Supply Co. at 1-800-292-5067 and they'll send you a catalog of all kinds of cool stuff for making your own jewelry.

Paper Cutting

Here are five trillion things to do with folded paper and scissors.

Paper Figures

Cut a rectangle of paper in half, lengthwise. Take one of the strips and fold *it* in half, widthwise. Fold the half in half. Now fold it once again. Open it up: you should have eight rectangular sections and seven creases. Begin to fold the paper like an accordion on the crease lines. At this point you can cut the folded paper in the middle, if you want to make small figures. (If you want to make a tall figure, leave your paper as it is.) Draw your figure, making sure that part of it touches each edge of the folded paper. Cut around your figures and unfold the paper. Draw features on each of your figures.

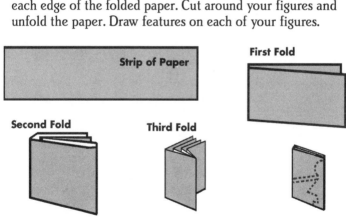

Repeat with the other strip of paper. Don't limit yourself to people: animals, buildings and trees are fun to cut out, too.

Paper Doll

Draw a figure on cardboard and cut it out. Or, cut a picture of a model out of a catalog, glue it to cardboard, and then cut it out. Now, take a sheet of paper and fold it in half, lengthwise. Draw doll clothes to fit your doll. Make sure the neck opening is at the fold and that it's big enough for your doll's head to fit through. Color the clothes, front and back. Cut them out and dress your doll.

Make a Pyramid

These make great ornaments. It's also a fun way to kill some time if you finish your test before everyone else. You'll need paper, scissors and glue.

Start with a rectangular piece of paper.

a.

Step 1
■ Fold paper in half, lengthwise (a).

Step 2
■ Open the paper and fold the lower right-hand corner up to a point in the middle of the paper (b).

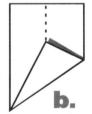

b.

Step 3
■ Bring the right-hand corner down, til it's even with the diagonal bottom line (c).

Step 4
■ Unfold the paper and cut on the folded lines (d). This is the shape you'll need to make your pyramid. At this point, it's useful to label the corners of your triangle (e).

c.

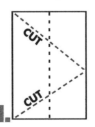

CUT

CUT

d.

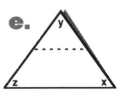

e.

Step 5
■ Fold X to the middle of the opposite side (f). Unfold.

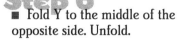

Step 6
■ Fold Y to the middle of the opposite side. Unfold.

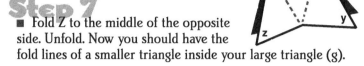

Step 7
■ Fold Z to the middle of the opposite side. Unfold. Now you should have the fold lines of a smaller triangle inside your large triangle (g).

Step 8
■ With X pointed up, fold the bottom of the triangle so that it looks like illustration (h).

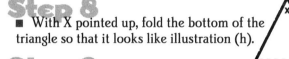

Step 9
■ Unfold, and do the same with the other two sides of your triangle (i).

Step 10
■ Now unfold the paper so it looks like illustration (j).

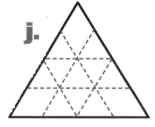

Step 11
■ Number the different triangles and make dark lines, as shown in illustration (k).

Step 12
■ Cut on the dark lines.

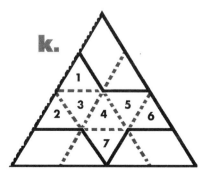

Step 13

■ Fold triangle 1 over triangle 5 and glue (l).

Step 14

■ Fold 2, 6, and 7 to make the base of your pyramid and glue them down.

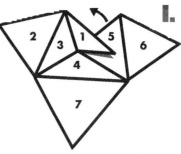

Now that you know how, try to make another one, this time without numbering the small triangles.

Make a Cube

One kid says, "You do a lot of folding, but it's pretty easy."

Step 1

■ Start with a rectangular piece of paper and make it into a square (a, b).

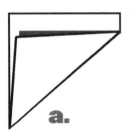

a.

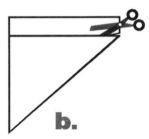

b.

Step 2

■ Fold another triangle (c, d).

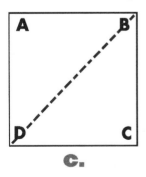

c.

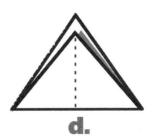

d.

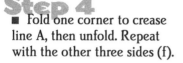

Step 3
■ Fold one corner to the center fold line, then unfold. Repeat with the other 3 sides (e).

Step 4
■ Fold one corner to crease line A, then unfold. Repeat with the other three sides (f).

Step 5
■ Fold each of the corners to the crease closest to it, then unfold. When you're finished, your paper should look like figure (g).

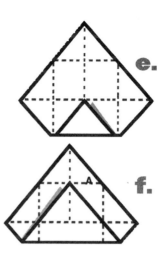

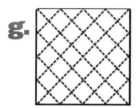

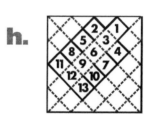

Step 6
■ Cut on black lines, as indicated by figure (h) If you want to decorate the sides of your cube, now's the time to do it. Keep in mind that not all of the squares will show once you assemble your cube.

Step 7
■ Fold into a cube. (There's no special way to fold your cube; any way you fold it, you'll get a cube!)

Now that you've got a cube, here are a few things you can do with it:

Make a 6-Sided Picture Puzzle: Make four cubes. Cut six different square pictures into quarters and paste one quarter of each picture on a facet of each cube. Do each block of four at a time, then mix them up and try to put them back together again.

Make a Holder for Your Ball of String or Yarn:
Glue all but one facet of your cube. Put in string. Make a
hole in the middle of each flap of the unglued facet, big
enough for your string to go through. Put string through
flaps, one layer at a time. Glue each flap to the one under it.

Make a 4-Color Cube Puzzle: This was a favorite
game of colonial American children. Make four cubes. Color
each facet of your cube according to the diagrams. The colors are red, white, blue, and yellow. (The box on the far right
side of each diagram indicates the bottom of each cube.) The
object of the puzzle is to line up all four cubes so that *each
one* of the colors is on all four sides in each row. (The end
colors count.) It can be done, but it's hard! If you want to
know the solution, go to the library and check out *Colonial
American Crafts: The School* by Judith Hoffman Corwin.

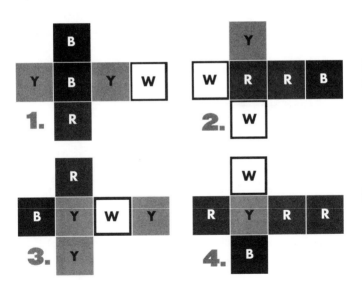

A Two-Color Lantern

Make a bunch of these out of brightly colored paper and
string them along a path to your house.

You'll need two different colored sheets of construction paper, scissors and tape.

Step 1
■ Take one sheet of paper and roll it, widthwise, into a tube. Tape shut at top and bottom.

Step 2
■ Fold the other piece in half, lengthwise (a).

Step 3
■ Make a series of slashes at the foldline, leaving borders at each end (b).

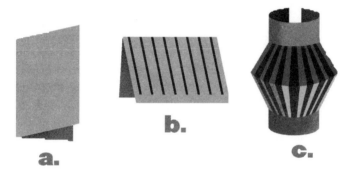

a.

b.

c.

Step 4
■ Open paper and wrap it around the other tube. Press it so the vents stick out (c).

Step 5
■ Tape the ends of the lantern together.

Step 6
■ Tape to the inner tube. Decorate the borders.

Step 7
■ Glue some yarn to the top, to hang your lantern.

Make a Paper Box

Use origami paper or a piece of wrapping paper, cut into a square.

Step 1
■ Fold paper in half, then fold in half again. Unfold.

Step 2
■ Fold all four corners to the middle (a).

Step 3
■ Fold two sides of the square to the middle, making a rectangle. Unfold (b).

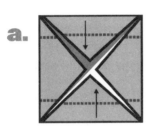

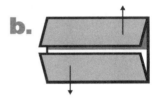

Step 4
■ Turn, and fold the other two sides to the middle (c).

Step 5
■ Unfold (d).

Step 6
■ Now, open two corners (e).

Step 7
■ Fold to the middle on the creased line (f).

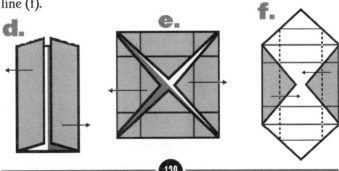

Step 8
■ Pinch the diagonal lines to the middle (g).

Step 9
■ Fold flap down (h).

Step 10
■ Repeat on other side (i).

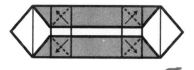

g.

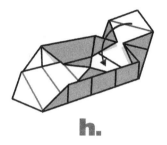

h.

i.

Nested Boxes

The perfect way to give a small, valuable gift to someone very special.

You'll need:

■ A pack of origami paper (If you can get a pack of different-sized paper, great. Otherwise, get a pack of the largest size.)

■ A pencil

■ A ruler

■ Scissors

Take the top sheet and put it aside. This will be the lid of your largest box. Take the next two sheets and, with a ruler, measure $1/2$ inch from the edge on all four sides. Trim off sides. Take the next two sheets of paper and measure 1 inch from the edges. Trim. Continue cutting off the edges, $1/2$" more each time, until you've reached a 5" square. (You only need to make one of these.)

Step 1

■ Make a box, as directed previously, with the largest piece of paper. This will be the lid of your nest.

Step 2

■ Repeat box-making steps 1 through 10, with all your paper.

Step 3

■ Now it's time to nest your boxes. Starting with the largest box, put all your boxes one inside the other. Put your present in the smallest box, then put the next-smallest box on top of it, for a lid. Continue to put bigger lids on each box until you run out of lids. Turn your nest-of-boxes over. Decorate the top box.

More Paper Fun

The Expanding Paper: Tell your friends that you can pass through a single sheet of paper. To prove it, do this:

Step 1

■ Take a sheet of paper and fold it in half, lengthwise. Cut along the horizontal lines, as shown in the picture. Cut *through* the fold for the lines that meet it. Cut from the outer edge *toward* the fold for the lines that meet the edge, but don't cut all the way across the fold!

Step 2

■ Open your paper up and fold it flat. Cut on the fold-line *inside* the paper, leaving about an inch on each end, as shown. Do not cut the fold-lines on either end!

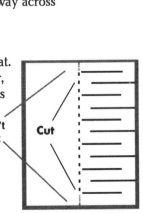

Step 3
- Open the paper up and step through it.

Shrinking Paper: A perfect way to send a secret message.

Step 1
- Take a piece of paper and write your secret message on it.

Step 2
- Fold paper in half, lengthwise (a).

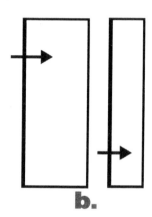

Step 3
- Fold in half again (b).

Step 4
- Take one corner of your folded strip and fold it to the edge, making a triangle (c). Continue folding into triangles (d) until you get to the last triangle before the top. Tuck top flap into the pocket of the triangle below it (e).

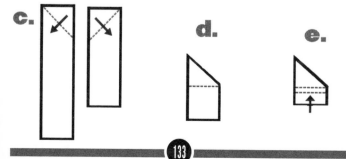

Printmaking and Painting

You can use everyday materials to make stamps for printing.

Cookie-Cutter Potato Stamps

Here's a variation on the old potato print. You'll need some cookie cutters with small designs: hearts, stars and animal shapes work well. Take a large potato and cut it in half. Blot the potato juice with a paper towel.

Press the cookie cutter into the potato, to a depth of about one-half inch. With a small, sharp knife, cut away the background from your design. Remove the cookie cutter. Pour a small amount of poster paint into a mini tray.* Put the roller into the tray and roll it back and forth until the paint is evenly distributed on the roller. Roll the paint onto the potato and stamp it on a piece of scrap paper. Adjust the thickness of your paint, if necessary. Now, stamp your design on stationery or craft paper.

*Most paint and hardware stores sell "mini-tray-and-roller" sets. They cost less than $3.00 and are definitely worth buying if you plan to do much printing. If you don't have one of these, just paint directly onto your stamp with a brush.

Glue Stamps

Draw a design by gently squeezing white glue onto a piece of corrugated cardboard. The small squeeze-bottles work best. Let your design dry overnight. Put some poster paint in a mini tray, spread it out and apply the roller to the raised glue design. Place some paper on the stamp and gently smooth it with your hand. Remove the paper and let dry.

Styrofoam Stamps

Take a good-sized piece of Styrofoam (not the small chips used in packing) and with a serrated knife, cut several blocks from it. With a ballpoint pen or nail, scratch a design onto one face of the block. If you're writing, be sure to do it backwards—you can double-check your writing by holding your stamp up to a mirror. Spread the paint evenly with a roller and make your prints.

Rubberband Monogram

Collect some wide ($^1/_8$") rubberbands. Cut them into strips and arrange them so they spell out your initials. When you're satisfied with the way your monogram looks, take a block of wood and lightly paint it with rubber cement. Make a border around the edges of the block, then place your monogram inside the border. Be sure to write your initials backwards, from right to left! Roll paint onto your stamp and use it to put your on ID books and other paper possessions.

Leaf Printing:

Make a scarf, a shawl, a tablecloth, or napkins by pressing painted leaves directly onto fabric.

You'll need:

■ Fabric (Natural materials like cotton, linen, wool, or silk absorb the paint best; if you're using wool, make sure it's soft and tightly woven.) If you're making a shawl, you won't need to hem it—just pull out a few warp threads, for fringe.

■ Fabric paint (Metallic paints like silver gold or copper look especially nice on dark fabrics.)

■ A paintbrush

■ Several leaves. Large ones with raised veins are best. Stiff, shiny leaves like oak or holly don't take the paint well. Make sure your leaves are freshly picked.

Gather your leaves and spread them out on newspaper. Have your fabric spread out nearby. Think first about where you want the leaves to go. (You may want to experiment by placing the unpainted leaves on the fabric.)

With your brush, paint a *thin* coat of fabric paint on a leaf. Carefully place it—paint side down—on the fabric. Cover with a paper towel and press it evenly with your hand. Remove and re-paint the same leaf (or a different one.)

When you've finished printing, "set" the paint by ironing it on the wrong side of your fabric. Follow setting instructions on your fabric paint jar.

Splatter Painting

You can make interesting prints with a wooden frame, some screen-door wire, a toothbrush, and paint or ink.

■ Pick up an orange crate* from a supermarket, and take the bottom slats off. Staple or nail a piece of screen wire to the top of the crate.

■ Place a leaf or some other familiar-looking object on a piece of white paper. Set this paper on newsprint, then put the frame over it.

■ Dip the toothbrush in paint or ink and rub it back and forth over the screen wire. The paint will splatter on the uncovered part of the paper. Remove the leaf from the paper and you'll end up with a reverse-stencil print.

*Or make a simple wooden frame by nailing four 2-by-4s together.

Make Splatter-Print Valentines
or Christmas Cards

Take a piece of white construction paper and fold it in half. Fold in half again, then a third time. Unfold the paper. It should be creased into eight sections. Now, take another piece of construction paper and fold it the same way. This time, leave the paper fold-ed. Draw a heart or a Christmas tree on the top section, and cut through all eight layers with scissors. Take your first paper and fold it in half, lengthwise, along the crease. Position it so that the folded end is on top. Four sections will be visible. Place a heart or tree in the middle of each section. Put the screen over the construction paper and splatter paint or ink on your cards. After removing the stencils, let the cards dry. Cut into four cards. Repeat with the remaining stencils.

How to Take a Good Picture

Whether you're using a disposable camera or a $10,000 dollar Hasselblad, the same principles apply when it comes to picture-taking: (1) have an interesting subject, (2) make sure the subject is well-framed, (3) have the right lighting.

Here are a few tips:

A good picture tells a story. It's one thing to take a picture of your friend's shoe. But if you get a picture of your friend's shoe right after he's stepped on a wad of chewing gum, your picture will be a lot more interesting. Even if it's a still life, try and have your picture convey more than one idea.

Keep it simple. Try not to have too much going on in your picture. If there are too many subjects doing too many things, there will be a "three-ring-circus" effect—the eye won't know where to go. Whatever your subject is—a person, a flower, a wad of gum—have a contrasting background: The background should either be lighter or darker than the subject. Your eye will naturally be drawn to a subject if it stands out against its background.

Keep it natural. A good picture doesn't look posed. When photographing people, give them something to do. If they're preoccupied, they won't look too self-conscious. Professional photographers always try to have some tricks up their sleeve when they go out on jobs.

Don't center your subject. Your picture will be more interesting if the subject is a little off-center. Also, try not to be on the same level as your subject, but shoot from a little above or below it. Angles and diagonal lines add excitement to a picture, so include them whenever you can.

Get as close as you can to the action. Your ability to get close to your subject depends on your camera's lens. Most automatic cameras don't feature close-up lenses, so experiment a little and discover just how close you can get, without losing focus. When taking portraits, it's not necessary for the person's entire body to appear in the shot, but be careful to leave some space above the subject's head. If you don't, the picture will seem "crowded."

Avoid These Common Mistakes

Tilted camera In general, try to keep your camera at the same angle (not level) as your subject. Diagonal lines are dramatic, but a tilted horizon can make the viewer feel a bit queasy.

Blurred image This happens when the camera moves at the same instant the shutter opens. Unless you're taking pictures on the Tilt-a-Whirl, keep your camera steady.

Bad lighting Lighting is what separates the amateurs from the professional photographers. You don't need a lot of special equipment like they do, but you do need some basic lighting tips.

■ Don't shoot directly into the sun. If you do, too much light will hit the film, and your picture will be washed out.

■ Keep the sun out of your subject's eyes. When you're shooting people, the sun should either be to their left or their right. If it is directly behind you, your subject will be squinting. If it is directly behind them, you'll be squinting and your picture will be over-exposed.

■ Avoid the midday sun when shooting outside. When the sun is directly overhead, it casts deep shadows under the subject. This is especially important when you're taking pictures of people. Morning or afternoon light isn't as intense, and makes for a better picture. Bright, overcast days supply the best light for shooting outside.

■ When using an indoor flash, try to limit the number of objects in your shot. Concentrate on your main subject, and try to keep the background simple. When taking flash pictures of people (or animals) you can avoid the 'pink-eye' effect by directing your subjects' attention away from the camera.

Parts of a Camera

shutter button — film advance — flash bulb

view finder — focus ring

lens

Things to Wear

Costumes

No matter how old you are, every girl needs to have some dress-up clothes handy for plays, festivals, theme parties, and Halloween. Your best bet for finding raw materials—at prices you can afford—is to look for rummage sales, thrift stores, and yard sales in your area. You can always find pre-owned gowns, shoes, evening bags, and jewelry to alter or wear as-is. Fabric stores usually have bins of left-over fabrics and trim at reduced prices, too. Don't limit yourself to fashion fabrics; you can make great costumes from bedspreads, upholstery, and curtain material as well.

Good, Cheap Stuff

Rummage and yard sales are usually held on weekends and are advertised in the local paper. Remember, at a yard sale, you can negotiate a price, just like in an open market. If a dress is marked "$1.00," but you don't think it's worth more than seventy-five cents, then offer fifty cents and see if the seller will meet you in the middle. If the seller won't budge, don't take it personally.

Thrift shops and second-hand stores have fixed prices, mostly. To find second-hand shops, look under "Thrift Stores" in the Yellow Pages.

If you need a costume in a hurry and don't have time to shop
or sew, you can always throw something together from
yardage—or an old bedspread, sheet, or curtain. Here are
some ideas:

A Wraparound Costume

This is an all-purpose wrap—good for portraying Greek,
Egyptian, or Biblical times. Use a lightweight material that
drapes easily. Your fabric will need to
be *at least* two yards (72") long and
one yard (36") wide. To deter-
mine the right length for a
floor-length costume, measure from right under your
arm down to the floor. Since
most fabric comes in 45 or
54-inch widths, you may
need to cut some material off
from the width. Start your wrap by
placing the fabric behind you, with both arms fully extend-
ed. Hold one corner of the material in your right hand. Bring
the fabric across the front of your body with your right arm
and pin it snugly to the material under your left arm.
Continue wrapping from left to right: across the front, under
your right arm again, behind and *over* your left shoulder. If
you have lots of fabric, let it drape there; otherwise, pin the
drape to the shoulder with a safety pin.

Circular Patterns

Whether it's a cape or a poodle-skirt, felt is the easiest
material to use with circular patterns because it doesn't
need to be hemmed.

A Half-Circle Cape

Measure the distance from your shoulder to your ankle. Take
that number, double it, and add another 12 inches. (For
example, if it is 45" from shoulder to ankle, you will need
102", or almost 3 yards, of felt.) Fold the material in half
lengthwise, then in half again. Using the folded corner as
your center line, mark off quarter-circles for the neckline
and hem with a piece of chalk tied to a string. The neck

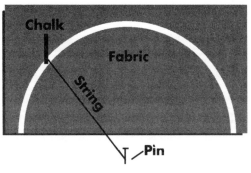

Center of Circle

should be 6" from the corner and the hem should be your measurement plus 6". Cut the cape out and sew two ribbons at the neck for ties.

'50s Poodle Skirt: These felt circle skirts were worn by girls in the 1950s. You can make a super-simple poodle skirt with two yards of felt, 72" wide.

■ Write down your waist measurement. (This is the number of inches it takes for a tailor's tape measure to go around your waist.)

■ Next, write down the number of inches from your waist to the middle of your shin.

■ Fold the felt in half, lengthwise.

■ Make a mark halfway along the fold (36").

■ Tie a long string to a piece of chalk, and hold it at the mark. Use the list below to decide what length string to use to make a circle the size of your waist.

  ■ If your waist is 18", the string should be 3" long from the mark to *end* of the chalk.

  ■ If your waist is 21", the string should be $3^1/2$" long from the mark to end of the chalk.

  ■ If your waist is 24", the string should be 4" long from the mark to end of the chalk.

■ Pinch the string on the mark at that length, and sweep the chalk around to make a half-circle. Add the string's length to your waist-to-shin measurement and let out the string to that number. Sweep the chalk around from the mark to (what will be) your hem.

■ Cut the felt on the chalk marks. Slash a 3" cut from the waist toward the hem. This should allow you to pull the skirt over your hips. If it doesn't, make the slash a little bigger.

■ Sew two ribbons on each side of the cut for ties.

■ Cut a poodle silhouette out of black felt and glue it to the front of the skirt.

A Medieval Cap

You will need:

■ A 12" x 24" piece of shiny material, like satin or brocade

■ A 12" x 24" piece of stiff backing, like buckram

■ Iron-on bonding material

■ $1/2$ yard of chiffon, to match color of cap

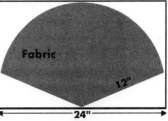

Lay the satin fabric on top of the buckram, and cut out a fan shape. With a large sheet of the iron-on bonding material between the two fabrics, "glue" the satin to the buckram. Roll the bonded materials into a cone and fit it to your head. Sew, staple, or glue the cap into a permanent cone shape. Attach the chiffon to the point and to one side of the cap. When the cap is on your head, bring the chiffon under your chin, and it pin to the other side, to keep the cap in place.

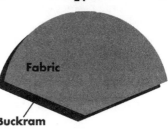

Make a Tu-Tu

You'll need:

- 2 yards of pink tulle (72" wide)
- 1 yard of ³/₄" elastic
- Scissors
- A needle and thread
- An iron
- A big safety pin
- An adult

Cut the tulle in half, lengthwise. You'll now have two 36" lengths. Have an adult iron the tulle flat, using a low setting. Fold each piece in half lengthwise and press again. By hand or with a machine, sew a straight line 1" from the fold, on both lengths of tulle. This is called a *casing*. Cut a piece of elastic 1" longer than your waist measurement.

Attach the pin to one end of the elastic. Thread the elastic through the casings on both pieces of tulle (the pin is your "needle"). Don't worry about sewing the two lengths of tulle together—there will be so many gathers in the fabric that the opening won't show. Making a ¹/₂" seam, sew the ends of the elastic together. Tuck the loose ends back into the casing. You'll end up with a very full tu-tu, 18" long. If you wish, make big zigzag cuts on the hem.

Ballet's Five Basic Positions

Patriotic Pleat and Dye

Before you take on a pleat-and-dye project with fabric, get the feeling of it first with paper towels and food coloring. Put about ten drops of red, blue, green, and yellow food coloring in four separate bowls. Add a quarter cup of water to each bowl. Take a strong paper towel (Bounty works best) and fold it in half. Fold it in half again. Keep folding into smaller squares until you have a small, tight square.

Now, dip the tip of one corner in red, one in blue, one in yellow, and one in green. Unfold and let dry. Your towel should be covered with different colored dots. Take another towel, and pleat it, accordion-style. Fold your long rectangle in half, then fold it in half again. This time, dip two sides of your square in the food coloring. Dip lightly, so some white remains in the middle. Unfold. You should have a row of stripes. The direction the stripes go depends upon which two sides you dip. Now, experiment by folding and dipping a paper towel in other ways.

When you feel comfortable with the pleat-and-dye technique, try it with fabric.

Make a red, white, and blue t-shirt

You'll need red and blue liquid fabric dye, a large paintbrush, a white t-shirt, a plastic bag, and a some rubberbands.

Put the red dye in one bowl and the blue dye in another. Starting from the bottom of the shirt, begin to accordion pleat it until you reach the neck of the shirt. Try to make your folds even. Fold the shirt in half, widthwise. The sleeves of the t-shirt will now be together. Slip a plastic bag over the sleeves only, and secure it tightly with a rubber band. Paint the edge of the folds *on each side* with red fabric paint. Make sure each fold is painted. These are your red and white stripes.

Open up the shirt and let it dry completely. Now for the "stars." First, make sure your hands are free from red dye. Take one sleeve, remove the plastic bag and begin to "tie-dye." Pinch a small amount of fabric together and wrap the tip tightly with a rubberband. Each tip will be a white star, so make sure it's covered. Make as many stars as you are able. Pinch and wrap both sleeves. When you're done, take one sleeve and—starting from the edge—dip it into the bowl of blue dye. Dip it only halfway—the dye will "bleed" up from the bowl, eventually covering the entire sleeve. When they have dried, unwrap the sleeves. Let the fabric paint set according to the instructions on the paint container.

Two Paper Airplanes

A Long-Distance Plane

Start with a square piece of paper:

- Fold the paper in half (a).

- Open and fold two corners to center. Crease (b).

- Fold both sides to the center again. Crease (c).

- Fold up center line, then fold the wings down (d).

- Point and throw.

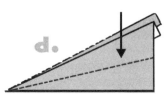

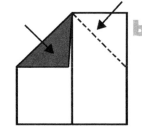

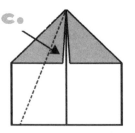

A Stunt Plane

Start with a rectangular paper.

■ Fold the paper in half, length-wise.

■ Open and fold the two corners to the center (a).

■ Fold the triangle down (b).

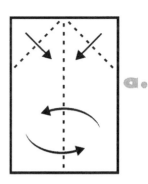

■ With the triangle pointing down, fold each corner to an imaginary point, 1" above the tip of the triangle (c).

■ Fold the tip up (d).

■ Fold the slanted edges, to meet at the middle crease (e).

■ Fold the wings up. Pinch at the folded triangle.

■ Point and throw.

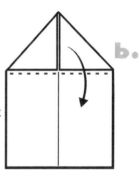

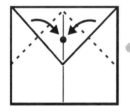

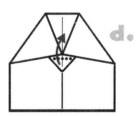

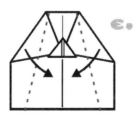

Fashion Magazine Fun

Tear out some pages with pictures of models from glossy women's magazines. (If you have a recycling area in your building or neighborhood, check it out for old magazines and catalogs.) With markers, draw mustaches, thick eyebrows, googly eyes, etc., on the pictures. Take a bunch of pages with you on your next car trip. See who can make the weirdest or funniest faces.

It's also fun to cut out male and female models from catalogs and make composites with them. You can glue a man's head on a woman's body, or vice-versa. Put workboots on a woman wearing an evening gown or high heels on a man in a double-breasted suit. Play Heads, Bodies, and Tails (see "Things to Do Indoors," page 160.) with magazine cut-outs. (Here it helps to have some old nature magazines, too.)

Catalog Paper Dolls

Find an old catalog and tear out a page with models wearing bathing suits or underwear. Paste the page to heavy paper. When it dries, cut the figure out. Next, cut out some clothes the same size as your paper doll. Make tabs at the shoulders and waist to keep the doll's clothes on. Don't forget accessories.

Fashion Designer Trading Cards

Design dresses and outfits and draw them on 3" x 5" index cards. Write the season or occasion your outfit is for (spring, summer, fall, holiday, active sportswear, etc.) and the name of your creation. Trade cards with your friends. Make accessory cards, too: shoes, hats, purses, belts, etc.

Wooden Clothespin Dolls

You will need:

■ Wooden clothespins (one piece, without metal clips—buy them in a large variety store, craft store, or craft catalog)

- Pipe cleaners—preferably white, pink, brown, and gold

- Yarn or cotton balls (for hair)

- Felt (for clothes)

- Glue

- Felt marker pens for eyes, mouth, shoes, etc.

First, make arms by twisting a pipe cleaner around the "shoulder" area. Some clothespins have indentations here, so these are the best ones to get.

Cut a piece (about 3" square) of felt, and make slits for the arms to poke through. Glue this "tunic" together in back.

To make a skirt, cut a 3"-round circle of felt and snip an opening in the middle for the doll's body to slip into. Or, make an A-shaped piece. You can experiment with all kinds of different costumes: a cape, tin-foil for a knight-in-armor, etc. You may also want to just color clothes on with your markers.

For the hair, cut 1" lengths of yarn and glue them to the top of the doll's head. For King and Queen dolls, make capes or crowns with gold pipe cleaners, or tin foil.

A Shoebox Dollhouse

When you look into a dollhouse, it's like entering a miniature world. Dollhouses are fascinating to kids and grownups alike; there are whole rooms devoted to them in museums all over the country.

- You don't need to spend a lot to have your own dollhouse—you can make one with four shoeboxes glued together. All the shoeboxes on each floor should be the same width, but they don't need to be the same length; after all, not all rooms are the same size. Whichever configuration you have on the first floor should probably be repeated on the second floor, though. You can even put a fifth box on top for an attic, and crown it with a slanted roof.

■ To connect the two floors, make stairs by cutting a long rectangle out of manila (file-folder weight) paper. With a stylus or one scissor blade, score a series of horizontal lines every half inch. Bend the paper at the score marks, to form steps. Cut a hole out of the second floor, right next to the dividing wall. The hole should be the same width as your stairs and big enough for a doll to fit through. Glue the stairs in place on the top and the bottom floors.

■ Once you have your structure, you can begin to furnish and decorate it. The two bottom rooms should be the kitchen and the parlor; the bed and bathrooms are upstairs. For wallcoverings, use contact or wrapping paper. (If you plan to use a patterned wallpaper, make sure it's a small one.) For the kitchen floor, use a small geometric pattern—like a checkerboard. To furnish your kitchen, paste magazine photographs of appliances onto empty spice or jewelry boxes. Glossy decorator's magazines like, *Architectural Digest*, are filled with pictures of rooms. From them you can cut out framed artwork, book spines, and lots of other details for your house.

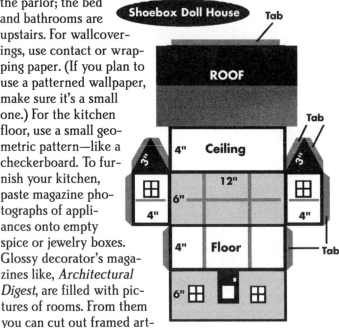

Shoebox Doll House

Tab

ROOF

Tab

3"   4"   Ceiling

12"

6"   4"   4"

4"   Floor   Tab

6"

(They can also provide you with beautiful carpets for your parlor and bedrooms. Some companies fill whole pages with photographs of their rugs.)

■ The next time you go the supermarket, start shopping for dollhouse furniture. Small medicine and spice boxes make great cabinets. You can paste cardboard shelves in them to display your books and knickknacks. Toothpaste boxes can be cut down to make kitchen appliances, tables, or cabinets. For your refrigerator, try using an anchovy-paste box. Use poster paint or tempura to paint over your box furniture.

■ Match boxes make great chairs (See the instructions, next page.) and dressers with sliding drawers. For handles, glue a bead to the front of each "drawer." Match boxes aren't as easy to come by as they used to be; still, many restaurants use them as advertising. Whenever you come across restaurant matchboxes, grab a handful! (Be sure you give any matches you've removed to an adult to store safely.)

■ Half the fun of having a dollhouse is furnishing it yourself. You can make tiny books, playing cards, and food from materials that you already have lying around your house. Supermarket fliers always have colored photos of boxes and cans of food. Cut these pictures out and paste them onto "boxes" made from cut-up wooden chopsticks. You can make cans by cutting wooden dowels into slices with a fine-toothed saw. If you don't have any wood trim at home, you can always pick some up at a hobby shop or hardware store.

■ Heat-drying clays like Sculpy and Fimo are perfect for making miniature food, vases, china, candles, and many, many other items. Also, most large hobby shops have a doll-house section. You can buy hard-to-make items there, like silverware, scissors, or birdcages.

■ If you don't have the right size dolls for your shoebox house, you can make dollhouse people from pipe cleaners and felt. Take one pipe cleaner, bend it in half, and twist a small circle at the top. This will be the head, neck, and torso of your doll. Take another pipe cleaner and cut it in half. Use one half to twist on the doll's arms at the "neck." Fold over the ends of the pipe cleaner for hands. Take the other half and twist it onto the torso, for legs. Cover the torso with felt clothes, and paste a magazine picture of a person's head on the front of the circle. Glue yarn or embroidery floss on the other side of the head, for hair.

Some museums that feature dollhouses . . .

The Museum of the City of New York; the Museum of Arts and Industry, Chicago; the Shelburne Museum, Shelburne, VT.

To Make a Chair From a Sliding Match Box

Use the part of the box that holds the matches. (Save the sheath for low cabinets or beds.) Turn the box over so that it sits on its rim. (See illustration.) Cut out three small

squares, for the spaces between the chair's legs. On the other half of the match box, cut off the three sides. Fold the "back" of the chair upward at the dotted line.

Doll Bed Linens

Make a comforter, pillow, and sheet for your own doll's bed, or as a present for your friend's doll.

You'll need:

■ ¹/₂ yard of cotton. Half will be for the sheets and pillow-case, and the other half for the comforter. If you'd like white sheets but a patterned comforter, get ¹/₄ yard of each. If you're using a print, make sure it's a small one.

■ ¹/₄ yard of white flannel

■ Cotton or polyester fill, for the pillow

- Needle and thread

- Scissors

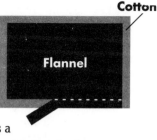
Cotton

Flannel

Comforter: The comforter should be several inches longer than the doll. Cut two equal-sized rectangles out of the cotton. Using one of the rectangles as a pattern, lay it on the flannel, and cut out the flannel. Pin the flannel to the wrong side of one of the pieces and sew around the rectangle, $1/2$" from the edge. (The *wrong* side of a fabric is the back of the side that's pinned to the pattern.

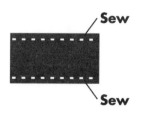
Pin both pieces together with patterns inside facing one another

With a print, you can tell the wrong side, because it's usually lighter in color.) With small scissors, cut the flannel close to the sewing line . With the flannel side facing down, pin the two "right" sides of the comforter together. Sew around three sides of the comforter. Turn inside out. Slip-stitch the remaining seam closed.

Pillow: From the remaining cotton, cut a piece 10" by 4". Fold the wrong sides together and sew up both sides. Turn pillow inside out and stuff it with the fill. Slip-stitch the end of the pillow closed.

Fold

Turn Inside Out

Sew

Sew

Stuff With Cotton

Sheets: Cut your remaining fabric in half. Make sure that you have an even piece. (Your sheet can be rectangular or square, but the width and length must be the same, on opposite sides.) Turn over one width end $^1/_4$ inch, then turn it over again. Sew it down. This is your top hem. Sew a smaller hem on the three remaining sides. *Hint:* If your doll is small, you can use a men's large white handkerchief for a sheet. You'll save yourself some hemming time. Make the pillow from another handkerchief.

A Clementine Crate Dollbed

Around Christmas time, you can find clementines—small, orange citrus fruits—in supermarkets and greengrocers. Buy a crate, and when you've finished eating them (they're delicious!) make a doll's bed from the empty crate. Sand the wood, then paint it a pretty color. Cut a piece of foam rubber the size of the crate and make a cloth cover for it. Put the doll's mattress in the box and make up the bed with your new linens.

Fly a Kite

Kites are more fun to fly if they're kites you've made yourself. Follow the pictured instructions:

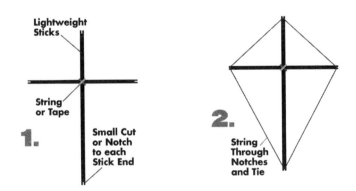

1. Lightweight Sticks · String or Tape · Small Cut or Notch to each Stick End

2. String Through Notches and Tie

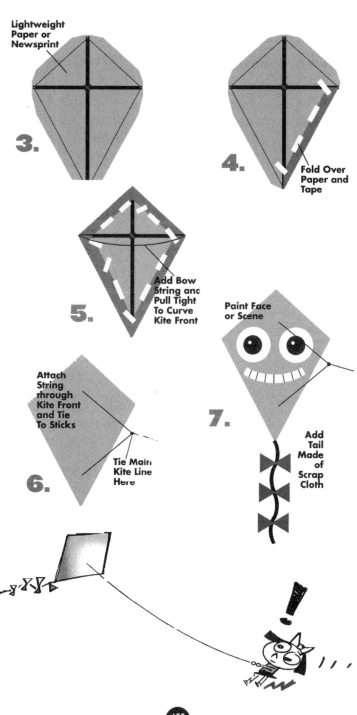

3. Lightweight Paper or Newsprint

4. Fold Over Paper and Tape

5. Add Bow String and Pull Tight To Curve Kite Front

6. Attach String Through Kite Front and Tie To Sticks

Tie Main Kite Line Here

7. Paint Face or Scene

Add Tail Made of Scrap Cloth

Patent Your Invention

If you think you've invented something totally unique, you may want to look into patenting it. When you patent something, you're registering it with the United States Patent Office—for a fee. This protects you from having your idea stolen. Once it's patented, you can sell your invention outright to a manufacturer, or work out a royalty agreement.

The first thing you have to find out is whether your invention is unique. Either you can hire someone (a patent attorney) to find out for you or you can do it yourself. Many large cities have patent libraries, where a record is kept of all past and pending (not-yet approved) patents. Patents are filed by category.

Once you're pretty sure your idea is unique, the next step is filing a patent application. There's a fee for filing an application, and no guarantee your application will be accepted. Still, if your invention is really terrific, it's worth it.

In addition to the fee, you'll need:

■ A document that describes your invention and explains how it is both unique and useful.

■ A technical drawing, which shows how it works

■ A notarized statement that you're the one and only inventor of your idea.

To find out about requirements and fees for patenting your invention, write:

Superintendent of Documents
US Government Printing Office
Washington, DC 20402

Ask for their guide, "Patents and Inventions: An Information Aid for Inventors."

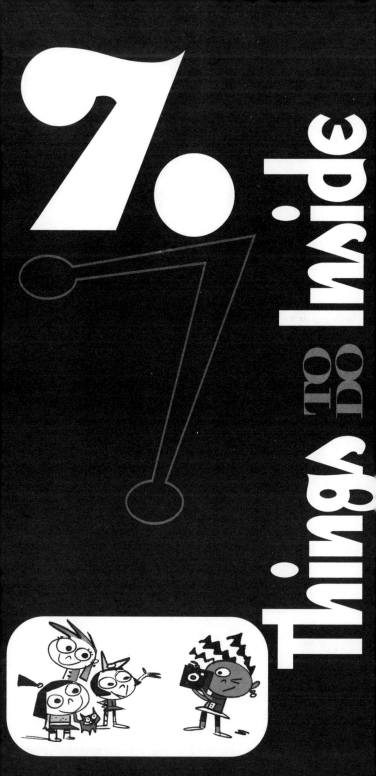

7.

Things TO DO Inside

Most kids would rather play outside. But you don't have to let a rainy day make your day a gloomy one. There's plenty to do indoors—even on a rainy day!

Games for Groups

Beanarino

Get three different-sized containers (for example, a cup, a cereal bowl, and a larger shallow bowl) and make a nest of the dishes.

Put the dish nest on the table, about four feet from the edge. Grab a handful of dried beans.

■ **The object** is to toss the beans into the bowls. If the bean lands in the biggest bowl, that's worth one point. If the bean lands in the middle-sized bowl, it counts for two points. And if the bean lands in the smallest bowl, it's worth three points.

DOIK!

■ **Each game is ten innings long,** and each player tosses five beans in each inning. The beans are thrown from behind the table (four feet away), one at a time, into the target. A player is allowed to lean over the table as much as she wants to, as long as she doesn't touch the table.

■ **After each player throws her five beans,** add up her score, write it down, and take the beans out of the dishes. Beans count only where they finally land. The player who scores the most points wins.

JQ

This is that little game—sometimes called "Hi-Q"—they sometimes put on tables in coffee shops. You can make your own.

Making the Board:
You'll need a block of Sculpy, Fimo, or any air-drying clay and a box of toothpicks. Roll the clay into a 4" square. It should be at least $1/2$" thick. Put a sheet of tracing paper over the pattern, right, and trace the dots onto the paper.

Put the tracing paper over the clay. With a toothpick, poke a hole through each dot into the clay. Bake or air-dry it until it's hard.

Setting Up the Game: Cut the toothpicks down to peg size and put a peg into every hole but the middle one. The object of the game is to "jump" your pegs, one at a time, until only one peg is left on the board. You can jump horizontally or vertically, but not diagonally.

Your first move will be over a peg and into the middle hole. Take the peg you've just jumped and put it aside. Now two holes are available and you have a choice of several possible moves. Continue jumping until you can't make any more moves. If more than one peg is left on the board, you lose. If only one peg is left on the board, you won.

Heads, Bodies, and Tails

■ Each player will need a pen and a piece of paper. Have each girl fold her paper into three sections.

■ Draw a head on the top third of the paper. It can be human or animal or anything you want—as long as it's a head. Draw a neck, making sure it extends into the second section. Fold your paper so that just the second section is visible and pass the paper to the person on your right. (The person on the left will pass her paper to you.)

■ In the second section, draw a body and arms—if your creature has them. Make the waistline extend into the third section. Fold the paper again—this time so that only the third section is visible—and pass it to the right.

■ Now it's time to draw the third section. The "tail" could belong to a fish or a reptile or a mammal or a Martian! When you've finished the drawing, fold your paper closed and pass it one last time. Everyone will get a laugh when they open up their composite drawings.

Charades

This is another game, like hopscotch, that many people play without actually knowing the official rules. Here they are:

■ You need at least six players for charades as well as scraps of paper, pencils, and a watch.

■ Divide the group into two teams. (If there's an extra girl, she can be the group leader and timer.) Give each girl a scrap of paper. Each player writes a familiar word or phrase. Almost anything goes. For example, you could write down a movie, a TV show, a book title, a song, the name of a popular band, or an advertising slogan. Since the object is to stump the other team, every player tries to make her word or phrase as difficult as possible.

■ The papers from each team are collected and put in separate piles or bowls. A player from Team 1 is given a paper prepared by someone from Team 2. The first player must silently act out the word, or words, on her paper. Her teammates try to guess what she's "saying." She is given four minutes. If her teammates correctly guess the message she's acting out, that team gets five points. If the time runs out, they get no points.

■ Whether or not the first team scores, the play now goes to the second team. A player from Team 2 is given one of the papers prepared by Team 1 and four minutes to act out the word or phrase. The teams take turns acting and guessing. Each girl gets a turn to act out a message for her teammates to guess. After all of the papers have been acted out, the team with the most points wins.

■ Before the game starts, the whole group needs to decide on gestures to represent the category each message falls in (a book, movie, song, etc.) They should also make up different gestures to signify "word," "group of words," and "syllable."

■ If you have a long word that's hard to act out, try breaking it down into syllables. For instance, "uncomfortable" could be broken down as "un" (the first syllable of onion), "come," "fort," and "table."

Pantomime

If you want to tell your friend, "That person over there is crazy" without the person knowing it, point your finger in the direction of the person and move it back and forth across your bared teeth, saying, "I brushed my teeth . . . " Now, move your finger around in a circle near your ear, and say ". . . and curled my hair."

Camouflage

Here's a fun indoor game for a group.

To set this game up, gather together about twenty small household items. Some possibilities might be a penny, a nail, a button, a sticker, a safety pin, a crayon, a walnut, a toothbrush, etc. When selecting your items, try and pick out things that will fade into the background of the room where they'll be hidden. (Try to pick out some things that are the same color as your sofa or rug, for instance.) Make a list of the items, and draw a blank line next to each item. Each player will need her own copy of the list. Now, go around the room and "hide" your items in plain sight. For instance, you might put a black button on top of a black book or place your walnut in the dirt of a potted plant.

Now you're ready to play. Assemble the group and hand each girl a check list. The players must find each of the listed objects. Tell them the items are not hidden, but they are camouflaged. When a player spots an item, she should check it off the list and write where it is hidden in the blank space, but *no player may move an object or in any way give away its hiding place.*

The first person to check off all the items gets a special prize, but the hunt continues until everyone is finished. It's not a bad idea to give everyone some sort of reward when she finishes. (If some kids are really having trouble, one of the finishers can help by telling them if they are "hot" or "cold.")

Put Her in Jail

It's like Hangman, except instead of hanging her, you put her behind bars.

One person's the guesser and the other person's the jailer. The jailer thinks of a word, say, "PEOPLE." The jailer makes six dashes on the sheet of paper; one dash for each letter of the words she's thinking of.

‾ ‾ ‾ ‾ ‾ ‾ ‾

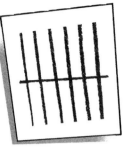

Next, the jailer draws the jail cell:

Now it's time for the guesser to begin guessing. If the guesser guesses the letter E, the jailer fills in all the E's.

‾ E ‾ ‾ ‾ E

But if the guesser guesses R, or some other letter not in the word, the jailer starts to put the guesser in jail. With the first

wrong guess, the jailer draws the guesser's head near the top of the cell. With the second wrong guess, the body; third wrong guess, a leg; with the fourth, the other leg; fifth, one arm; sixth, the other arm.

After seven wrong guesses, the jailer locks the guesser in jail, by drawing bars across the guesser. The jailer then picks

another word and the game starts all over again. But if the guesser guesses the word in time, she becomes the jailer.

Murder!

This is a game to be played in the dark of night:

Each player draws a piece of paper from a paper bag. After looking at her paper, each person crumples it up and tosses it back in the paper bag. Most of the papers are blank. But one paper has "Murderer" written on it and one other says "Detective."

The Detective leaves the room and the lights are turned out. Make sure the room is very dark. The rest of the players move around in the middle of the room until the Murderer puts her hands on somebody's throat. That person screams and drops to the floor.

Turn the lights on and call in the Detective. The Detective asks questions, which everyone has to answer honestly— everyone but the Murderer, that is, who's allowed to lie.

By asking clever questions, the Detective tries to figure out who the Murderer is.

Marbles

■ **Ringer:** With chalk, make a large circle on asphalt. Make two crossing lines, dividing the circle into quarters.

■ To decide which player goes first, have each kid shoot a marble towards the center. The player who gets closest to the center cross goes first. The next closest goes second, and so on.

Cracked Marbles

Here's a fun thing to do around the campfire or at a cookout. You'll need some marbles, a cup of cold water, and an old wooden spoon. Heat a marble in the coals of a dying fire. When the marble is somewhere between very warm and hot, scoop it up with the spoon and drop it in the cup of water. The marble will crackle inside but stay intact. If your marble is too hot, though, it will crack into pieces. You'll probably need to experiment with a few marbles until you get it right.

■ **Next, each player places her marbles** in an *L* shape, on the outside of each of the four quarters. If there are only two players, place your marbles across from each other in two of the quarters. Each player should have an equal number of marbles to start with.

■ **The first shooter aims** her boulder from any spot on the edge of the ring. Any marble that she knocks out of the circle belongs to her. She keeps shooting until she fails to knock a marble out. Now, it's the second shooter's turn. She also keeps shooting, until she misses. The game continues in this way, until all the marbles have been knocked out of the ring. The player with the most marbles at the end wins.

Marble Golf

This game needs to be played on tightly-packed dirt. With a stick, draw a large circle on the ground. In the very center, dig a hole (If you want, you can put a small cup in the hole.) Scatter the marbles evenly, inside the circle. Each player takes turns trying to knock marbles into the cup. When a marble is knocked in, the player gets to keep it. The first player keeps shooting, until she misses; then, it's the next player's turn. The game continues until all the marbles have been knocked into the hole.

Soda Bottle Bowling

You can do this indoors or out. You'll need:

- 10 2-liter plastic soda bottles, with caps.
- Sand
- A funnel
- A tennis ball, softball, or baseball

Put the funnel in a soda bottle. Fill the bottle a third of the way up with sand. Screw on the cap. Fill the remaining bottles in the same way. Set up the bottles as shown below and have each player try to knock down as many as possible in three throws.

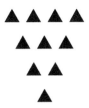

Broom Hockey

Simple—brooms for hockey sticks, boxes or laundry baskets as goals, and a nerf or other lightweight ball for a puck. Better clear this with a parent first.

Pickup-Sticks

Also known as "jackstraws," pickup-sticks is a game that is played in one form or another all over the world. In one version, you let the fifty sticks fall willy-nilly on a table. The object of the game is to remove the sticks, one-by-one, without disturbing the others. You can buy a set of them, but they're a cinch to make, too. Just take 50 wooden kebob skewers and, with food coloring, dye them different colors.

To score the game, give the various colors different values. For instance, you can make five red sticks, worth ten points each; eight blue sticks worth 5 points each; twelve green sticks worth 3 points each and the rest of the (undyed) sticks can be worth 2 points apiece.

Acting Up

It's fun to put on plays for friends and family. Try making a play out of one of the stories or books you already know or love.

Peter Pan, by Sir James M. Barrie, makes a great play. You, of course, get to choose your favorite role. If you have younger brothers or sisters, they can play the other kids.

Start with chapter three, where Peter comes into the children's bedroom, to find his lost shadow. Peter's shadow can be a piece of black chiffon tied to fishing line. (Have someone make it fly around the room by pulling on the line from offstage.) Tinker Bell can be the light of a flashlight shining on the wall. If you have some tinkly chimes, play them whenever Tinker Bell speaks.

Other suggestions: *Nancy Drew* mysteries; the play the March girls perform in *Little Women*; musicals like the *Wizard of Oz*. It's fun to act out the Greek myths, too.

It's in the Cards

Hearts

This is a fun card game for three or four players. The object of the game is to get rid of all the hearts you're holding in your hand, and to keep from getting new ones. In the end, the player with the least number of hearts wins. (If, a player has managed to pick up *all* the hearts, however, she wins the game. This is called "shooting the moon"—see warning, below.)

The deck of cards is dealt face down to all the players. (If there are three players, put the extra card to one side.) The player to the left of the dealer leads by placing a card (any suit but hearts) face-up in the center of the table. The player to her left must then follow suit by putting down a card of the same suit. Play continues to the left until everyone has played a card. The player who puts down the highest card of that suit must take all of the cards—which is called "winning the trick." (She must also take the left-over cards, if there are any.) If a player has no cards of the leading suit, she may then put down any card she likes, including a heart. (Once this happens, hearts have been "broken.") This is the time to get rid of any hearts or high cards, because a trick may go only to the highest card in the *leading* suit. The girl who wins the trick then leads the next one. The round is finished once all the cards have been played.

To score, each girl adds up her hearts. Every heart is worth one point, except the queen of hearts, which is worth 13 points. (To add a little variety to the game, you can use other cards instead of the queen of hearts. For example, you might declare the 10 of spades equal to 11 points and the 2 of diamonds equal to 2 points.) Players decide ahead of time whether to play to 50 or 100 points. The first player to reach the agreed-upon number loses. At that point, the player with the lowest score wins.

Warning: Only an experienced player should attempt to shoot the moon. If a player is clever enough to do it, however, she may deduct 26 points from her total.

What Beats What in Poker

Poker: a great way to double your allowance, if you can get your dad into a game. Here's the list, from the best poker hand down to the lowliest. For example, a straight flush beats four of a kind, and four of a kind beats a full house, and so on.

■ **Straight Flush:** Five cards in numerical order and all of the same suit. If you have an ace, king, queen, jack, and 10 of the same suit, that's called a royal flush, the best poker hand you can get.

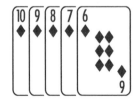

■ **Four of a Kind:** Four cards, all of the same denomination. There will be one unmatched card left over.

■ **Full House:** Three cards of one denomination, and two cards of another denomination.

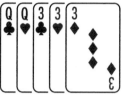

■ **Flush:** Five cards all of the same suit (for example, all diamonds, all spades, all hearts, or all clubs). The cards don't have to be in sequence,or order.

■ **Straight:** Five cards in sequence, but not all of the same suit.

■ **Three of a Kind:** Three cards all of the same denomination, and two unmatched cards.

■ **Two Pair:** Two cards of one denomination, two cards of another denomination, and one unmatched card.

■ **One Pair:** Two cards of the same denomination, and three unmatched cards. A higher pair always beats a lower pair.

■ **High Card:** Five unmatched cards. If no one has any of the above, whoever has the highest card (starting, from the top, with A, K, Q, J, 10, 9, and so on) wins.

The "Dead Man's Hand"

Aces and eights are called the dead man's hand because that's the hand that Wild Bill Hickok was holding when he was shot in the back!

A Card Game You Can Make

This game is called "Authors." Count out fifty two cards from a package of 3" x 5" index cards. Divide your "deck" into thirteen sets of four cards. Think of thirteen authors you've heard of and some books that he or she has written. (You can also use playwrights, poets, or movie directors.)

Take the first card from the first set and write the name of an author in large letters near the top of the card. Above the author's name, write the title of one of her books. Under her name, write the names of three other books she has written. Above the author's name on the *second* card in the set, write one of the three other books she has written. Under her name, write the names of the other three. Repeat with the third and fourth cards in the set, putting the name of a different book at the top of each card. Prepare each of the twelve remaining sets in this way, using a different author for each set of four.

After you've made all fifty two cards, shuffle them and divide them up between three to six players.

The object of the game is to collect as many sets as you can. When it's a player's turn, she might ask one of the other players, "Do you have *Emma* by Jane Austen?" If that player is holding that card, she must give it to the asker. If she gets the card she asks for, the first player takes another turn. If she's holding the three other Jane Austens, she puts all four cards down on the table, saying "I have a book." If an player *doesn't* get the card she asks for, it's the next player's turn.

Index Card Gymnastics:

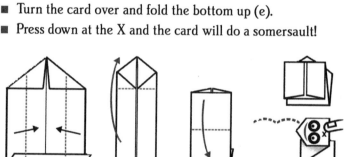

■ Take a 3" x 5" index card and fold it in half, lengthwise.

■ Unfold, and fold two corners to the middle (a).

■ Fold up the bottom, as pictured (b).

■ Fold both sides to the middle (c).

■ Fold the top over, at the dotted line (d).

■ Turn the card over and fold the bottom up (e).

■ Press down at the X and the card will do a somersault!

Two Good Card Tricks

Trick One

You'll need a table and a tablecloth.

■ Display four overlapping aces on the table. After your audience takes a look, whisk the cards together and stick them in the middle of the deck.

■ Ask someone in the audience to shuffle the cards. Show the audience you don't have any cards in your hands or up your sleeve. After the cards have been well shuffled, ask the shuffler to put the deck on the table.

■ Invite the audience to come and hunt for the aces. They'll only find three—the ace of diamonds won't be in the deck. Pick up the deck and whack it on the table, saying, "I knocked the ace through the table!"

■ Lift up the tablecloth and show everyone the missing ace.

Here's how you do it:

The trick is that the audience never really saw four aces on the table—the ace of diamonds was hidden all along. The cards you showed at the beginning were three aces and the nine of diamonds.

Arrange the cards so that an ace is on each side of the nine, and the audience can see just the central diamond:

Make sure the audience doesn't look too closely at the cards when you're going the trick. And as soon as you can, push the cards together and put them in the deck.

Trick Two

■ Hold up four spread out kings. Push the kings together and put them on top of the deck of cards, which you should be holding in your other hand. Lift the top king off the pile, show it to your audience and say, "I'm putting the first king on the bottom of the deck." Then do so. Without showing the next card take it off the pile and announce, "The next king goes in the middle of the deck." Put it in the center and do the same thing with the following card, but make it very obvious that the third card is not close to the card you have just placed in the middle of the deck.

■ Take the fourth card, show it to the audience, and say, "I'm keeping this last king on top of the pile." Cut the cards and put them on the table. Ask someone from the audience to cut the cards again.

■ Now say something like, "You've seen me put kings in different parts of the deck. The deck has been cut twice—once by someone from the audience. Now I'm going to bring the kings together." Hit the cards with your fist, and ask someone from the audience to look through the deck: All the kings will be together.

Here's how you do it:

Take the four kings and two jacks out of the deck. Put the two jacks behind one of the kings. Make sure the jacks are absolutely hidden behind the king—keep the edges flush.

■ When you fan the four kings at the beginning of the trick, make sure the king with the hidden jacks is the second card from the right as you spread the cards. Be careful not to show the jacks! When you turn the cards over and bring them together, this will be the order of the cards: king, jack, jack, king, king, king.

■ Put these cards on top of the deck. Pick up the first card—a king—and show it to everyone in the audience before you put it on the bottom. Since the next two cards are jacks, make sure you don't show them as you stick them in the middle of the deck. Even if the audience gets a glimpse of the cards, they'll assume they're kings, since jacks are picture cards, too.

■ After the jacks are safely buried in the deck, show the audience the next king, but tell them it's the last king. With the first cut of the deck, the king that's on the bottom of the deck will be brought on top with the other three kings, putting all the kings together. The next cut (from the audience) should put the kings somewhere in the middle of the deck. Good luck!

Pitching Cards

Two people, a deck of cards, and a hat—that's all you need for this one!

Divide a deck of cards into red (hearts and diamonds) and black (clubs and spades) suits. One player uses red cards, the other black cards.

Put the hat upside down on the floor. Pick and mark a place about five feet away from the hat. Each player takes turns pitching cards. Three cards are pitched on each turn. On the last pitch, only two cards are pitched.

When no more cards are left, count the number of cards that made it into the hat and you'll have a winner.

Rainy Day Fun

Cookin' Up Fun

Here are the recipes. Now it's up to you.

Snowp: Mix equal parts Ivory Snowflakes and water. Beat with an egg-beater until stiff. *Warning*: snowp looks and spreads just like cake frosting.

Bubbles: Mix together two cups of clear liquid dishwashing detergent, $3/4$ cup of Karo syrup, 6 cups of water, and (if you have it) a few drops of glycerin. Mix well, and blow.

Silly Putty: Fill a plastic food container one fourth of the way up with white (Elmer's-type) glue. Add a few drops of food coloring, and stir. Add some liquid laundry starch until the container is half full. Stir again. (The mixture will begin to solidify and cling to the spoon.) Add more starch, until the container is almost full. Take the putty out and knead it with your hands until it is soft and rubbery. Drain off any extra liquid. To keep it pliable, store Silly Putty in a Zip lok bag.

Gloop: In a plastic food container, combine 1 cup of white glue with $3/4$ cup of hot water. Set aside. In another bowl, combine 1 tablespoon of Borax with $1/2$ cup of hot water. (Borax can be found along with laundry powder in most supermarkets.) Add half the Borax solution to the glue container and knead for a few minutes. Add the other half and continue kneading, until the mixture solidifies. Drain off any extra liquid. When it is not in use, store the gloop in a Zip lok bag.

Permanent sculpting sand: Measure 4 cups of sand, 2 cups of cornstarch, and $2^{1}/2$ cups of water into an old pot and heat on a low setting until the mixture becomes thick. Sculpt, and let your creation air-dry. Extra sand may be stored in a Zip lok bag.

Stained glass: Measure $1/4$ cup of hot water into a cup. Add several drops of food coloring, and stir. Gradually, add 2 packages of plain gelatin to the water, stirring as you do. When all the gelatin has dissolved, pour the mixture into two plastic food container lids. Allow it to dry overnight. The "stained glass" can be cut into different shapes with scissors. *Hint:* After a few hours of drying, shapes can also be cut out with cookie cutters.

Scented stained glass: Follow directions as above, but use flavored and colored Jell-O instead of gelatin and food coloring.

Homemade glue: Measure 4 cups of water into a large saucepan and heat to a boil. While the water is heating, measure $1/4$ cup of cornstarch into a cup. Slowly add $1/2$ cup of cold water, and stir until there are no lumps. When the water boils, add the cornstarch and water to the pan. Stir until the mixture becomes clear. Cool, and store in a plastic food container.

Two Yo-Yo Tricks

Sleeper

This is the trick where the yo-yo stays in one place, or "sleeps," while it's spinning.

Hold the yo-yo in your hand, palm up. Now bring your arm up to your shoulder, just like you're making a muscle.

Snap your hand downward, and at the same time relaxing your hand so the yo-yo will land gently. What you're trying to do is reduce the friction between the axle of the yo-yo and the string. If there's too much friction, the axle will grab at the string and start its return spin back into your hand.

If you're able to reduce the friction, your yo-yo will sleep. The next thing you'll have to figure out is how long to let the yo-yo sleep before you make it come back to your hand. That's something you'll learn with lots of practice.

Walking the Dog

To walk the dog, first you have to be able to throw a fast sleeper. The faster your sleeper, the longer you can walk your dog. After throwing a fast sleeper, very carefully swing the yo-yo out, making sure it lands gently. The force of the spin will make the yo-yo walk along the floor or ground, with you trailing behind it.

As with the sleeper, you have to make sure to tug the yo-yo back into your hand before it stops spinning.

Who Invented the Yo-Yo, Anyhow?

The yo-yo comes from the Philippines, where it started out as a weapon. Early Philippine jungle inhabitants tied vines or animal sinews (tendons or muscles) around grooved rocks, and used these to knock animals—or human enemies—on the head. If they missed with the first throw, they could yank the rock back with the vine or sinew, and try again. "Yo-yo" comes from a Philippine word meaning "to return."

Growing a Crystal Garden

You will need:

- Charcoal briquettes
- Salt
- Bluing (sold in the laundry detergent section of stores)
- Ammonia
- Food coloring
- Small glass jar, cup, spoon, measuring spoons

Put a couple of charcoal briquettes in a small glass jar. In a cup, mix together 1 tablespoon of salt, 1 tablespoon of water, 1 tablespoon of bluing, and 1 teaspoon of ammonia. Pour the mixture over the charcoal briquettes. Sprinkle a few drops of food coloring on top. Put the crystal garden in a safe place and watch it grow.

Map Making

On a rainy day when you're stuck inside, you can always pass the time charting the great outdoors. Make a map of your neighborhood, using the private names you've given various locations. For example, if you call the house two blocks over the "mean lady's house," that's the name you'll put on your map. If you make a map of the route you take to school, put in the shortcuts and show which neighbors' yards and pets are best avoided.

It's fun to do this on graph paper because the squares make it easy to keep things in scale. Don't forget to make a key for your map—you can used the symbols shown on the next page, or make up your own.

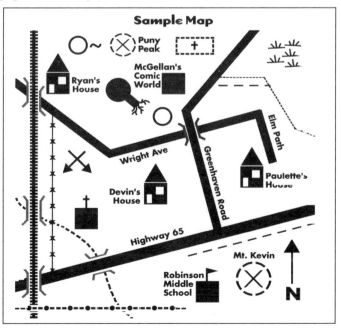

Commonly Used Map Symbols

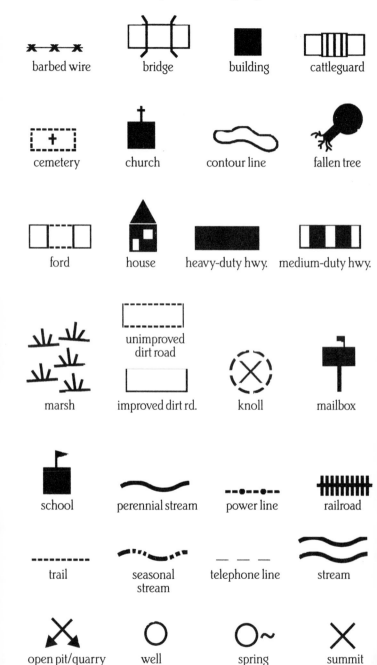

barbed wire	bridge	building	cattleguard
cemetery	church	contour line	fallen tree
ford	house	heavy-duty hwy.	medium-duty hwy.
marsh	unimproved dirt road / improved dirt rd.	knoll	mailbox
school	perennial stream	power line	railroad
trail	seasonal stream	telephone line	stream
open pit/quarry	well	spring	summit

Internet Surfing

If you get your parents' permission, you can explore the Internet for games, pictures, sounds, movies, and freeware.

Use a search engine such as WebCrawler or Magellan, for example, and put in the keyword for a subject you are interested in.

Pictures Say you want to get the logos for college sports teams. Type the keyword "sports," the name of the college you're interested in and/or the college's nickname (Example: "Wolverines"). This should get you mighty close to the logo.

Sounds Type in the subject you like and the word "sound" and/or "audio." One fun thing to look for is downloads from your favorite cartoons and movies.

Movies When looking for movie clips, your best bet is to type in the subject you like and the word "QuickTime." QuickTime is the most common way movies are stored on the Internet.

Freeware Freeware is software available on the Internet and, believe it or not, it's free. You'll find games, programs for doing art and movies and for creating animations, among many other things. When you're searching, put in the word "freeware." This word should give you a list of sites that offer free programs.

Before you download anything, make sure you have an anti-virus program! You can download a free one called SAM DIS-INFECTANT.

On-line Lingo & Faces

Once you get on the Internet you're sure to see some of these abbreviations:

IMHO: In my humble opinion

LOL: Laughing out loud

ROTFLOL: Rolling on the floor laughing out loud

BTW: By the way

B4N: Bye for now

FWIW: For what it's worth

<g> grin: This lets the person you're "talking" to know you're kidding about something.

You may also find these faces (turn your head sideways) made with the keys on the keyboard.

:-)	:-D
;-)	: - (

These are called "emoticons," a word made from two other words— "emotion" (because the little faces show how you're feeling) and "icon" (because icons are small symbols used in place of words).

If you need help with your homework and you're on America On Line, type in the keyword "homework." Teachers are standing by to help. You can also find homework help on the Internet by typing "homework" into a search engine.

Be an Armchair Traveler

You can get great books, pamphlets, brochures, and maps from foreign countries by just asking for them! Here's the way to get the mail rolling in:

First, find some travel magazines. Check the periodical (newspapers and magazines) section of your library. Since periodicals often can't be checked out, bring a pen and a notebook with you. In the back of each travel magazine, you'll find a section that offers free brochures from travel agencies, suggesting exotic places to visit.

Write down their addresses (or 800 numbers, if they have them) and ask for whatever they're willing to send you. In addition to travel agencies, you can also get information from local and foreign governments. Each state in the US has a department of travel and tourism, and most countries do, too. Ask the librarian to show you how to find addresses for these. Also, ask for the out-of-town phone books. Every city and town has a Chamber of Commerce, and you can write to them and ask for promotional materials— travel agencies and bureaucrats are eager to tempt you with pictures, maps, bumper-stickers, decals, or postcards, all for the asking, and a stamp.

Collect cities, states, and countries. Trade with your friends. See how many different islands you can get, or how many countries in each continent. So, sit back and wait for the mail to come rolling in. Your friends will be surprised when they see the kind of mail you're getting— and they'll be impressed with your stamp collection, too!

Get a FREE beginners stamp collection packet from:

Junior Philatelists of America
P.O. Box 850
Boalsburg, PA 16827

Rain Gauge

The official rainfall is determined by the amount of rain that falls in one cubic inch of space.

You can make your own accurate rain gauge. You'll need a 1" beaker—available at a hobby shop or a chemistry supply store. If your beaker isn't marked, get nail polish and label it yourself. Measure it out in $1/4$" segments.

Next, wire the beaker to a small board. Make sure the wire isn't too tight—you have to be able to get the beaker in and out when you empty it.

Now attach the board (nail or wire it) to a pole or fence post that's totally exposed to the sky on all sides. After each rainfall, check (and empty) the beaker-gauge.

For a free science catalog that sells beakers and lots of other science supplies, write to:

Edmond Scientific Company
Science Division
101 East Gloucester Pike
Barrington, NJ 08007-1380

Phone: 1-800-728-6999
M–F 8 A.M.–P.M., Sat. 9 A.M.–4 P.M.
Fax: 1-609-547-3292
E-Mail: scientifics@edsci.com

Connect the Dots

Here's a fun strategy game. You and your opponent both share the "board." Take a piece of paper and draw 16 dots, arranged like this:

```
•   •   •   •

•   •   •   •

•   •   •   •

•   •   •   •
```

In this game you take turns drawing a connecting line between any two dots. In each turn you may connect *only* two dots. You can put your line anywhere; it can be horizontal (straight across) or vertical (up and down), but not on a diagonal (slanted).

The object of the game is to make as many small squares as you can, within the large square. If you connect the fourth line to make a square, you "capture" a box. Then you get to put your initials in the box, and take another turn. The winner is the girl who has claimed the most boxes at the end of the game. This game is a little like chess, because you need to think a few moves ahead to win. Try not to be the one to put the third line on a box; you'll be setting up your opponent to score.

If you want to play longer, make a 36-dot square—6 rows of 6.

Wordplay

Use these expressions to impress your teachers and friends:

■ You're pressing upon my neural transmitters in a deleterious manner.
(Translation: You're getting on my nerves.)

■ I beg to differ. On the contrary . . .
(Translation: You're wrong! It's like this . . .)

■ Please forgive my oblivescence.
(Translation: Sorry. I forgot.)

■ I am currently experiencing a eudaemonistic state.
(Translation: I'm so happy!)

■ Would you please reiterate that statement? I was experiencing omphalokepsis.
(Translation: What'd you say? I wasn't listening.)

■ Although I covet her leiotrichous condition, I would readily eschew her lentiginous epidermis.
(Translation: I wish my hair were straight like hers, but I'm glad I don't have her freckles.)

■ I fear that you have been less than forthright and obfuscated veracity.
(Translation: You lie!)

■ He excels in philematology.
(Translation: He's a good kisser.)

FYI

■ If a word ends in "mania" it means a type of *madness*.
■ If a word starts with "philo" or ends in "phile" it means *a lover of*.
■ If a word ends in "ocracy" it means *a government of*.
■ If a word ends in "ology" it means *the study of*.
■ If a word ends in "mancy" it means *a way of predicting the future*.

Zodiac Code

This Zodiac alphabet was used by alchemists, astrologers, and philosophers during medieval times. They hoped, by using it, to keep their knowledge secret. As codes go, though, it's not too complicated. It's a straightforward substitution code—each letter of the alphabet is represented by the symbol next to it in the chart below:

A	⊙ Sun	J	☾ Moon	S	Capricorn
B	Jupiter	K	Taurus	T	Fishes
C	Saturn	L	Twins	U	Ram
D	Neptune	M	Cancer	V	Aquarius
E	Uranus	N	Lion	W	>
F	⊗ Earth	O	Virgo	X	≫
G	♀ Venus	P	Libra	Y	H
H	♂ Mars	Q	Scorpio	Z	<
I	☿ Mercury	R	Sagittarius		

Morse Code

Morse Code

People don't send message by telegraph anymore, which is what Morse Code was invented to do, but there are lots of other uses for this code. A message can be tapped out on a wall, beaten on a drum, whistled out, blinked out at night with a flashlight, or flashed with a mirror in daytime, using the sun.

Here's How Morse Code Works: Each letter of the alphabet has a signal made of dots and/or dashes. Dots are short, and dashes are three times longer than dots. No matter how you send your message, by flashlight or by tapping, this will always be true.

Just count to 1 for a dot and to 3 for a dash.

For example: A = • —   Z = — — • •
Count: 1; 1-2-3   1-2-3; 1-2-3; 1; 1

Morse Code

A • —	J • — — —	S • • •	1 • — — — —
B — • • •	K — • —	T —	2 • • — — —
C — • — •	L • — • •	U • • —	3 • • • — —
D — • •	M — —	V • • • —	4 • • • • —
E •	N — •	W • — —	5 • • • • •
F • • — •	O — — —	X — • • —	6 — • • • •
G — — •	P • — — •	Y — • — —	7 — — • • •
H • • • •	Q — — • —	Z — — • •	8 — — — • •
I • •	R • — •		9 — — — — •
			0 — — — — —

Samuel Morse, the inventor of Morse Code, also came up with a way to memorize the code. Look on the next page for a list of words that Morse came up with to go along with his code.

As you can see, the word picked for each letter of the alphabet begins with that same letter (except for two). And each word has as many syllables as each code letter has dots and dashes. The long syllables in each word are dashes; the short syllables are dots.

A	Ag-ainst	•—	J	Ju-ris-dic-tion	•———	S	Se-ver-al	•••
B	Bar-ba-ri-an	—•••	K	Kan-ga-roo	—•—	T	Tea	—
C	Cont-in-ent-al	—•—•	L	Le-gis-la-tor	•—••	U	Un-i-form	••—
D	Dah-li-a	—••	M	Moun-tain	——	V	Ve-ry va-ried	•••—
E	(short)	•	N	Nob-le	—•	W	Wa-ter-loo	•——
F	Fu-ri-ous-ly	••—•	O	Off-ens-ive	———	X	Ex-hi-bi-tion	—••—
G	Gal-lant-ly	——•	P	Pho-tog-raph-er	•——•	Y	Youth-ful and fair	—•——
H	Hu-mi-li-ty	••••	Q	Queen Kath-a-rine	——•—	Z	(two long, two short)	——••
I	I-vy	••	R	Re-becc-a	•—•			

When you've memorized these twenty-six words, you've also memorized the Morse Code.

Invisible Ink

■ Lemon juice makes an excellent invisible ink. Cut a lemon in half and squeeze the juice into a small dish. Use anything that has a point—a dried up pen, the wrong end of a match, etc. Dip the point into the "ink," but don't use too much, or else the paper will wrinkle. Printing is usually easier to read than cursive.

■ To make the message visible, hold it up to a lightbulb.

■ Milk can also be used for invisible ink.

■ Another good idea is to write your message between the lines of an already-written letter. The hidden message will turn up when the paper's exposed to heat, and the original letter or note will serve as a decoy.

Hiding a Code Book

The best hiding place is an unexpected one. Tape your code book to the bottom of your waste basket, then put crumpled paper over the code book. A small code book can be hidden in the pocket of a jacket or coat that's hanging in your closet. Cut a square hole in the middle of an old book to make a secret hiding area for your code book.

And if your enemies are closing in and you need a fool-proof hiding place, you can always send your code book to yourself in the mail. That will give you a couple of days breathing room to find a new, secure hiding spot.

Collecting

There's almost nothing that people won't collect—glass eyes, string, barbed wire—you name it and someone probably has a house full of it. Museum basements all over the world are jammed with people's collections. It would take another book to make a complete list, but here's a collection (in no particular order) of *just a few* of the things that kids like to collect:

Rocks, seashells, seaglass, butterflies, acorns, leaves, coins, stamps, rubber stamps, postcards, playing cards, baseball cards, stuffed animals, glass animals, comic books, heart-shaped boxes, Pez dispensers, dolls, candles, keychains, keys, cat figurines, dog figurines, any-animal figurines, pens, pencils, pencils with town names on them, erasers, boyfriends, yarn-loop-chains, business cards, toothbrushes, Barbies, bugs, pictures of snakes, pictures of white tigers, pictures of horses, anything to do with horses, hair, rings, candy wrappers, cans, buttons—and that's just for starters!

Two Unusual Things to Collect

A Spider Web Find an abandoned spider web. Spray the web with hair spray. Press a sheet of black construction paper on the web. The web will stick to the paper.

A Twig Alphabet Twigs grow in all kinds of shapes. Find ones that form letters. Ys and Vs are easy to spot, but if you look closer, you'll find other letters. You can combine several twigs to make tricky letters like Q or R. Glue your twig alphabet to a large piece of posterboard and mount it on a wall.

Indoor Rainbow

This only works on a sunny day.

If your mother will let you borrow her diamond ring for just a few minutes, try rotating it in the sun to make an instant rainbow. If she says "no" to the ring idea, try this one:

Find a table that's directly in the sun. Fill a glass of water almost to the top. Carefully put it on the edge of a table so that it half off the table. Put a sheet of blank, white paper on the floor beneath the glass. Keep fiddling with the paper and glass until you get the angle right for a rainbow.

What Makes a Rainbow?

Although sunlight looks white or yellow, it's really red, orange, yellow, green, blue, indigo, violet all mixed together. A rainbow is simply white light that has been bent in different angles by raindrops. The drops of water separate the colors.

A prism, such as the diamond ring, bends light, turning ordinary daylight into a rainbow of color. To see a rainbow outdoors, you have to have both rain and sunshine.

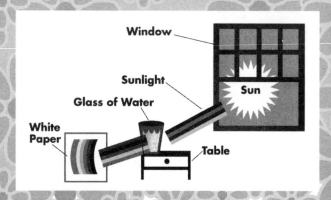

8.

Things to Outvine

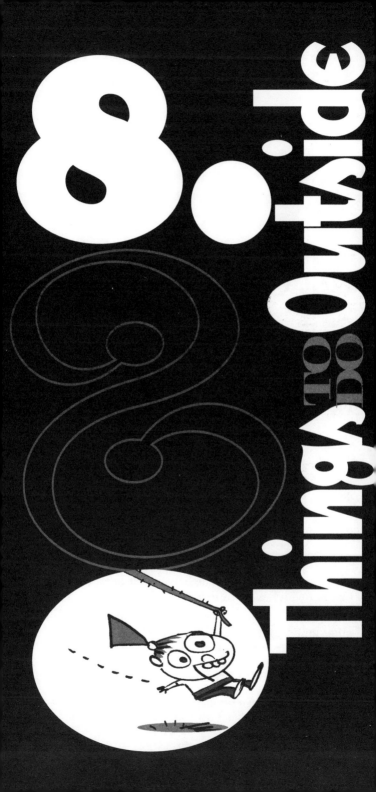

Once upon a time, kids who stayed at home were called "homebodies." But then, as now, most girls enjoyed knowing how to have fun outside the home as well as they did inside it. All it takes is mastering the basics.

Sports & Games

Baseball

How to Throw a Baseball

The hardest thing to remember about throwing is that you throw with your whole body, including your arm and shoulder, not just with your arm and wrist.

■ Extend your arm far backward. Don't bend your arms sharply at the elbow. The elbow should be behind you, not sticking out in front.

■ As you bring your arm high over your head, begin striding forward with the opposite foot.

■ As your arm comes forward in a whiplike motion, the other foot comes forward. Immediately after the ball is released, your feet should be parallel again.

How to Find the "Sweet Spot" on Your Bat

Hang a baseball on a piece of string from the edge of a porch or table. Hold your bat with your thumb and middle finger

Who Goes First

Odds and Evens: One person calls "evens" or "odds." Both make a fist, and on the count of three, show one or two fingers. If both of them show the same number of fingers, evens win. And if one person shows two fingers and the other shows one finger, odds win.

Baseball Bat: One player grabs the middle of the bat. A player on the other team grips the bat above the first player's grip. They alternate grips, one hand above the other, until there's no more space on the bat. Whoever is holding the top of the bat wins.

For Three or More Players: Odd finger is It—everybody makes a fist. All players say, "one, two, three, shoot," then, like "Odds and Evens," above, show one or two fingers. Keep doing this until someone shows a different number of fingers from everyone else. That person becomes it.

so the bat hangs down and swings, using your fingers as a pivot point. Let the bat swing gently against the dangling baseball. Not hard, though. When you find the spot where the bat doesn't vibrate at all when it hits the ball, you've found the sweet spot. It's usually about three to six inches from the fat end of the bat. In a game, if you hit the ball on this spot, it'll really travel.

The Infield Fly Rule Explained

The point of this rule is to keep the defensive team from making a double play by deliberately dropping an easy pop to force out a base runner.

Here's how it works: With runners on first and second base and fewer than two outs, a batter who hits an easy pop to the infield is automatically out.

The runners may proceed at their own risk—but, generally, they do so only if they're stupid.

Important Things to Know About Soccer

Here is a very nice thing to know when you want to play soccer on a team that has boys on it—be really tough and fight for the ball because girls are stronger and bigger than boys at your age.

■ At the beginning of the game, one team is on one side, and the other team is on the other side. You try to kick the ball in the net which is on the other team's side.

■ Always wear shin guards to protect your legs.

■ Wear a short-sleeved shirt because when you run, you get really hot.

■ When you're dribbling the ball with your feet, keep the ball close to you so no one will steal it.

■ If you have long hair, put your hair in a ponytail so you can see the ball and what's going on in the game.

■ If you're a goalie, stay close to the goal so you can grab the ball if it gets too close to the net.

■ Don't touch the ball with your hands if you're not a goalie, or the referee blows the whistle and the other team gets the ball.

■ If the ball goes out of the lines, the team that didn't touch the ball last gets to kick it back in.

■ Don't eat too much candy before the game or else you will get a stomach ache when you try to run.

■ Keep your eye on the ball even if you see a cute guy on the sidelines.

■ Be nice to the other players even if they make faces at you.

■ Practice hard with your big brother or sister at home so you can do well in the game.

Your Personal Olympics

To hold your own Olympics, you need to come up with five or ten events.

You might have a high jump, a long jump, hurdles, a throw for accuracy (throwing a ball through a tire), a distance throw, a bicycle race, a javelin throw (a stick of pampas grass makes a great javelin)—anything you can think of. Of course, you'll need a running event!

You'll need timers and tape measures. When you set up your events, make sure there's enough room to throw or run without hitting each other or a neighbor, and check that long-jumpers have a soft place to land.

Record the first-, second-, and third-place winners. Keep track of the scores. First place: 5 points; Second place: 3 points; Third place: 1 point.

How to Make Gold, Silver and Bronze Medals

You'll need plaster of paris (available at any hobby store); a plastic yogurt cup, and straw for each medal you make; and silver, gold, and bronze spray or model paint.

Stick
or Pen

Straw

Mix up the plaster of paris according to the direction on the package, and pour a little bit—about $^1/4$"—in each yogurt cup. (Some kinds of yogurt have a top that is just about the right depth.)

Olympic
Symbol

Yogurt
Lid

Stick your straw near the edge of the cup; you're making a hole to put the ribbon through.

You might want to cut the straws into smaller pieces, so they don't topple over. Before the plaster dries completely, use a marker top or an old pen or stick to impress the five Olympic rings on your medal.

When the plaster of paris dries, peel the yogurt carton away and push the straw out—you should have a hole near the top now.

Spray or paint each medal gold, silver, or bronze. Put a ribbon through the hole and you have real Olympic-style medals!

Backyard Obstacle Course

This is pretty good fun for two to 20 kids. If you're raising money for your school or church, you can charge 50¢ for each kid to go through the course. Have someone time how long it takes each kid to run the course, and give a prize to the fastest.

Every obstacle course is different, because every back yard is different. You'll need to take advantage of your yard's special features. Here are some ideas for obstacles you can set up:

Obstacle 1: Island Hopping
Round up as many large buckets as you can and have the runner step in each one, without tipping any over. If a bucket tips, make the runner start again.

Obstacle 2: Mountain Climbing
Set up a series of sturdy sawhorses, ladders, or benches for the runner to climb over.

Obstacle 3: Swinging Through the Jungle

If you have a tree in your yard, tie a rope swing to it. Have the runner swing out and land in a designated area (an old throw rug, for instance). If you don't have a tree, set up a broad jump.

Obstacle 4: Mystery Caves

Get some large corrugated boxes—the kind appliances come in—and connect them together with gaffer's tape. Put in some dead ends, if you can. Attach some fringed material (like car-washes have) for the runner to pass through.

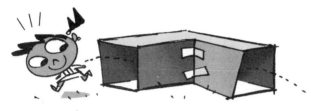

Obstacle 5: Crossing Piranha River

Find a long ladder, and set it flat on the ground. The runner must step on each rung, without slipping. If one foot slips off, the piranhas get it, and the runner becomes a hopper. (If both feet slip, she's out.)

Obstacle 6: Whirlpool

Coil some low garden fencing (or strips of corrugated box material) into a whirlpool shape. Make it just wide enough for one foot to step through at a time. If the fence tips over, the runner must go through whirlpool again.

Obstacle 7: Army Ant Stamp Take some bubble wrap (large bubbles are best) and cut it into even-sized pieces. Cut one piece for each runner. Have the runner pop every bubble in her sheet, before she can proceed to the next obstacle.

POP!

Obstacle 8: Under the Falls Have someone hold a garden hose with the nozzle held up, so there's a narrow arch for the runner to pass through.

A Clock Putting Green

You don't need acres and acres of fairway to work on your golf game. All you need is your lawn, a sharp stick, a piece of string, twelve golf tees, and a tin cup. Let your folks know what you're up to, because you'll be digging a hole in the middle of your homemade golf course.

■ **First, ask an adult to mow the lawn as closely as possible for you.** (You might want to offer to rake the lawn first to soften up the adult.) Estimate where the middle of your lawn is, and put the wooden stick in that spot. Next, take a 24' piece of string, and mark its middle (at 12'). Tie the string to the stake in the middle. Think of the circle that the string makes, as it sweeps around the stake, as a big clock.

■ **Find 12:00 and mark it with a tee.** Make a straight line to the opposite side, and mark 6:00 with another tee. Next, mark 3:00 and 9:00 the same way. Fill in the other "hours" with tees, until you have a circle that is divided into twelve even sections. Remove the stake and dig a hole at the center spot. Put a small tin cup in the hole. (The top of the cup should be at ground level.) Now that your golf course is set up, you're ready to play.

■ **Starting at 1:00,** try to hit the ball into the cup in two shots (*par*). If you do, move on to 2:00. Your entire course will be par 24. See how close you can get to par, as you travel around the clock. If you're playing with others, proceed as above. If you fail to get the ball into each cup in two tries, though, let the second player take his turn. Continue in this fashion, until all of you have hit "around the clock." If you want to get fancy, you can create some obstacles, and make some shots harder than others.

Stilts

Wood Stilts

You'll need two pieces of wood, each about 2" wide, 1" thick, and 2' longer than you are.

Use two pieces of board for foot rests. Cut the foot rests at a slight angle into two equal shapes, as shown in the picture.

The higher you put the footrests, the taller you'll be.

Attach the foot rests to the stilts with three screws.

Tin-can Stilts

Large juice cans work especially
well. Using a hammer and nail,
punch two holes in each can on
opposite sides about an inch down.

Now string some sturdy cord (the length
depends on how tall you are) through
the holes and up to waist height, tying
the two ends together with a strong finishing knot. Repeat
the procedure for the other can and you're ready to do some
can stilt-walking.

Lawn Games

Mother, May I? Put two lengths of brightly-colored
yarn on opposite ends of the yard, making a "start" and a
"finish" line. One girl (the caller) stands behind the finish
line, and the rest of the group (the runners) stand behind the
start line. The caller chooses a runner by name, saying
"Bridget, take two giant steps forward." Bridget then says,
"Mother, may I?" to which the caller can either say "Yes," or
change her mind and say, "No. Take two scissor steps
instead." (Or baby steps, hops, backwards steps, forward
rolls, or anything else she can think of.) Bridget then takes
the required steps. The caller continues down the line of
runners, asking for various steps. She can mix the steps up
(one giant step forward, two baby steps back, for instance),
but each runner must move forward, each time—even if it's
just a tiny bit. If a player forgets to say, "Mother, may I?" she
has to go back to the beginning. The first player to cross the
finish line becomes the next caller.

Red Light, Green Light This game is set up the same
way as "Mother, May I." The caller yells, "Green light!" and
turns her back to the runners, who run forward as fast as
they can. After a few seconds, the caller yells, "Red light!"
and spins around. If any of the runners is still in motion, she
must return to the start line. The first runner to cross the
finish line becomes the next caller.

Red Rover Divide the group into two teams, with both teams facing each other about fifty paces apart. The players on each team link arms. In Red Rover, each player gets a chance to be a caller, in turn. (You can start at one end of the line and move down towards the other end.) The first caller yells to the other team, "Red rover, red rover, let Rachael come over." Rachael breaks away from her line, and charges toward the opposite team's line. If she's able to break through it, she gets to return to her own team. If not, she must join the opposite team. The game continues until all the girls are on one team (or everyone gets bored with the game).

Kick the Can You put a tin can in the middle of a little circle about a yard across. One girl is *It*. One of the other kids kicks the can as hard as she can kick it, and the girl who is *It* has to count to ten slowly, then go get the can and put it back into the circle. Meanwhile, everybody else runs and hides. The kid who is *It* has to try to find one of the other kids. As soon as she sees a girl who is hiding, she has to yell, "I see you!" and the name of the kid she sees. Then they both race to the can. Whoever gets there first immediately kicks the can again. The kid who gets there second has to go and get the can (but this time, she doesn't have to count to ten), put it in the circle, and go look for the kids who are still hiding.

Follow the Leader This one dates back hundreds of years, but it's amazing how many kids have never played it. The more, by the way, is always the merrier.

Nothing could be simpler. Everyone follows after the leader, doing exactly what she does, going wherever she goes. Over walls, up trees, down alleys, through tunnels.

You don't have to be a great athlete to be a good leader, but you should have a good imagination. The best games of follow the leader have both easy and hard stunts. As a leader you can also do funny walks, somersaults, or slither like a snake—virtually anything you dream up.

Tag

In most tag games, one person is chosen to be *It*. *It* chases the other players, and anyone who is tagged then becomes *It*. Here are some other tag games:

Grass Tag: This game is played on dirt fields where there are occasional patches of grass. Runners are safe from *It* as long as they are touching grass.

Shadow Tag: Runners are safe as long as they're in the shade, but they can be tagged in sunlight.

Nose-Toe Tag: Runners are safe only when they pinch their noses with one hand and hold a toe with the other.

Freeze Tag: When a player is tagged, she must remain frozen into position until one of her teammates can "unfreeze" her by touching her.

Marco Polo

You play this in the swimming pool. The object of the game is for the person who's *It* to catch other players while her eyes are shut tightly. *It* goes to the middle of the pool and everyone else swims around her. She tries to find the other swimmers by calling out "Marco" When she does this, everyone else has to shout out "Polo," which gives away their locations. Once a player is caught, she becomes *It*.

Jackstones

"Jacks" was originally played without a ball, and stones were used rather than the star-shaped jacks we're familiar with today. The game was called "Jackstones." You can still play this game with five smooth stones or acorns, if you don't have any store-bought jacks on hand.

Here's how to play Jackstones: Scatter five jacks onto a hard surface. Pick up one, throw it into the air and—with the same hand—quickly pick up another jack, while the first is still in the air. Catch the first jack, again with the same hand. Put one jack to the side, and continue in this way until all of the jacks have been picked up, one at a time. This is called "onesies."

After onesies, you play twosies, picking up two jacks at a time. Next, you pick up three at a time, then the one remaining jack. Finally, you pick up all four jacks, while the fifth is in the air. If you miss or drop a jack, or if you touch any jacks you aren't picking up, you forfeit your turn. If you're playing alone, this means you must start again from the beginning. If you're playing with others, it means that they get to go, until they win or forfeit their turns. When your turn comes around again, you pick up where you had left off last time.

Regular Jacks is played with the same rules as Jackstones, except there are more jacks and you use a ball. (The ball is bounced, and while it's in the air, you pick up the jacks.)

Knock, Knock goes like this: bounce your ball, pick up a jack and knock it once on the table, before catching the ball. Next, knock two times—then three—until you fail to catch the ball.

A Superball

Take a jack, and wrap a rubber band tightly around its spokes. Continue wrapping rubber bands in, out and around the spokes of the jack, until it is completely covered in rubber. You can make your superball as big as you want. When it bounces, rubber bands will go flying off around the room.

Hopscotch

Everybody knows how to play hopscotch, but very few girls know how to play it the right way.

For this sidewalk game you'll need some chalk and a marker to throw into the boxes.

Keychains make excellent markers, but you could also use a stone, a shell, a beanbag, or a bottle-cap. With the chalk, draw a long rectangle, then divide it into twelve sections, as pictured here.

Boxes 1, 4, and 7 should be slightly over one foot-length wide.

Standing behind the starting line, throw your marker into box 1. With one foot, hop into the box. Jump completely around so you're facing the starting line and kick the marker out. Hop out. Next, throw your marker into box 2. Hop into box 1 with one foot, then into boxes 2 and 3 with both feet. Jump completely around, and kick the marker back into box 1. With one foot, hop into box 1, then kick the marker over the starting line. Continue this way, advancing one box at a time, then retracing your hops until you've made it all the way to box 12.

If you miss a box with your marker, or step on a line, you lose your turn to the next girl. She then plays until she reaches 12 or forfeits her turn. When your turn comes around again, you pick up where you left off.

When you make it to box 12, kick your marker out the other way and write your initials in any box you choose. This becomes your box and the other players are not allowed to jump in it. *You* may, though—with both feet, if you choose. The game continues until it becomes impossible to jump from one free box to the next, or until all of the boxes have initials in them. The girl with the most boxes, wins.

Make a Beanbag

It's easy. Just take two pieces of material cut exactly the same size and shape. (You can make a plain square one or you can make fancy shapes like butterflies or shamrocks.) Sew them together along all the edges except one because you have to leave an opening to put the beans into the bag. Fill up the bag with dried navy beans or dried peas or dried corn or even small pebbles. Then sew up the opening.

Jump-Rope and Hand-Clap Songs

You can't learn jump-roping or hand-clapping from a book. You just have to have someone show you. Big sisters have been showing their little sisters how to do it since before your great-grandmother was a girl. Here are some songs that have been around for longer than anyone can remember. Some of these are hundreds of years old!

Hand-Clapping Verses

Virginia* had a baby,
She named him Tiny Tim.
She put him in the bathtub,
To see if he could swim.
He drank up all the water,
He ate up all the soap.
He tried to eat the bathtub,
But it wouldn't go down his throat.
Virginia called the doctor,
The doctor called the nurse.
The nurse called the lady
With the alligator purse.
"Measles!" said the doctor.
"Mumps!" said the nurse.
"Lifebuoy!" said the lady
With the alligator purse.

Out went the doctor,
Out went the nurse,
Out went the lady
With the alligator purse.

*Sometimes "Miss Lucy," not to be confused with "Miss Lucy had a steam-boat . . . ," which everyone knows. The verses of "Miss Lucy" are too rude to print here.

Down, down, baby;
Down the rollercoaster.
Sweet, sweet baby,
I'll never let you go.
Shimmy-shimmy cocoa-pop,
Shimmy-shimmy, pow!
(2 times)

Gramma-gramma sick in bed,
I called the doctor and the doctor said:
Let's get the rhythm of the head (ding-dong) *(2 times)*
Let's get the rhythm of the hands (clap-clap) *(2 times)*
Let's get the rhythm of the feet (stomp-stomp) *(2 times)*
Let's get the rhythm of the H-o-t dog (swivel hips) *(2 times)*
Put it all together and what do you get?
Ding-dong; clap-clap; stomp-stomp; h-o-t dog!
Put it together backwards, and what do you get?
D-o-g hot; stomp-stomp; clap-clap; dong-ding!

Jump Rope Verses
Teddy bear, teddy bear, turn around;
Teddy bear, teddy bear, touch the ground;
Teddy bear, teddy bear, tie your shoe;
Teddy bear, teddy bear, now skidoo!

Johnny over the ocean,
Johnny over the sea,
Johnny broke a teacup,
And blamed it on me.
I told Ma,
Ma told Pa,
Johnny got a lickin'
Ha, ha, ha!

Salt, vinegar, mustard
And don't forget
The red-hot-pepper! *(double-time)*

Cinderella
Dressed in yella
Went upstairs
To kiss her fella
Made a mistake
And kissed a snake
How many doctors did it take?
One-two-three, etc. *(Count until there's a miss.)*

Fudge, fudge, tell the judge
Momma has a brand-new baby;
It isn't a girl and it isn't a boy
It's just a big old baby.
Wrap it up in tissue paper,
Send it up the elevator:
First floor, miss!
Second floor, miss!
Third floor, miss!
Fourth floor—open door!

Not last night but the night before,
Twenty-four robbers
Came knocking at the door.
As I ran out to let them in
This is what they said to me:
Lady, lady, turn around;
Lady, lady, touch the ground;
Lady, lady, make a kick;
Lady, lady, do the splits!

Beachcombing

The best time to go beachcombing is when the tide is low.
That's when you can collect all kinds of treasures the high
tide has left behind, like shells, seaweed, crabs, jellyfish,
driftwood, sea glass— sometimes even jewelry and money!

There are two high and two low tides every twenty four hours, but their times vary from one day to the next. Check the local paper to find out the times of the high and low tides.

High and low tides are caused by the gravitational force of the moon. The moon pulls the water away from Earth, the way a distant magnet pulls on metal filings. The part of Earth that is closest to the moon will experience a high tide. On the opposite side of the world, there will also be a high tide, but for a different reason: because the force of the spinning earth is pushing water away from its surface. When tides are highest in one part of the world, they are lowest in another.

The absolutely best time to go beachcombing is right after (not during!) a storm. When the ocean gets churned up, all kinds of neat stuff is thrown onto the shore.

"Spring" and "Neap" Tides

Once every month, the tide is especially high. This is because there is an extra force pulling on Earth's water: the sun. When the sun, moon, and Earth are lined up, the gravitational pull is increased and more water is pulled away from Earth. These extra-high tides are called "spring" tides. Because the high tides are higher, the low tides become even lower during this period.

A spring tide is a great time to go beachcombing.

When the sun and the moon are at a 45° angle to Earth, the moon's gravitational pull is at its weakest. The difference between high and low tides is less pronounced during this period. This phenomenon is called a "neap" tide.

Beachcomber's Lamp

At any large hobby shop or lighting store, you can buy a "bottle assembly kit." These kits cost around $7 and include all of the stuff (cork, wire, plug, and socket) you'll need to turn a bottle into a lamp. Collect enough small shells and seaglass to fill a clear wine bottle. Follow directions on the kit.

Outdoor Creations

Vine Fort

This will take a month and half or so to grow into a real fort, so start as soon as you can.

In a sunny part of the yard or garden, make a circle of short, wooden stakes. Put the stakes about a foot apart, except for the "doorway," which should have a couple of feet between stakes.

Pound a very tall pole or stake in the middle of the circle. String twine from each stake to the top of the pole. At this point, your "fort" will look like a string teepee.

Now plant pole beans at the bottom of each wooden stake. As the beans start to grow, wind them around the string. By the time the beans reach the top of the pole, you'll have a terrific fort. Don't forget to water your fort!

Branch Lean-To Fort

You'll need a tree with a fork, a long branch or pole, and lots of shorter branches and sticks.

Stick the long branch in the fork of the tree, so that you have a triangle shape.

Now take your shorter branches and lean them against the main pole. Cross-hatch the branches or sticks so that you'll have a framework for lacing in more branches for maximum coverage and camouflage. Do it on both sides.

Leave room for a door!

How to Make a Daisy Chain

Pick some daisies, dandelions, or wild asters. Make sure the stems are at least 1" long. With your fingernail, make a slit near the top of the stem. Slide the next flower into the slit, then make a slit in that flower. Continue making the chain until it's long enough to go around your hair or neck. To close the circle, make a longer slit in the last stem, then push the head of the first flower through it.

Flower

Slit

Stem

Beaded Daisy Chain

You'll need:

- Seed and bugle beads
- Strong thread
- A needle with a small enough eye to go through beads
- Scissors

- A clasp and jump-ring
- Glue

First, decide which two colors your want to use for the daisies, and which color for the chain. For each daisy, you'll need eight seed beads of one color and one seed bead of another color. Each daisy should be separated by three bugle beads. Sort the beads and put them in three containers. When one girl made her daisy chain, she chose white for the outside of the daisy and yellow for its inside bead. She used black bugle beads for her chain. Here's how she did it:

Step 1
- Put a long (arm's length) thread on a needle.

Step 2
- Tie the clasp on the end. Double knot it.

Step 3
- String on three black beads and eight white beads.

Step 4
- Bring the needle around to the first white bead and put it through the hole closest to the black bead.

Step 5
- String one yellow bead and bring the needle through the fifth white bead (the hole closest to the sixth bead).

Step 6
- Pull tight. (The white beads should surround the yellow bead. If they don't, it means your needle went through a bead in the wrong direction. If so, unstring beads and try again.)

Step 7
- Repeat steps 3 to 6. When your chain is as long as you want it to be, tie a jump ring onto the end. Double knot it.

Step 8
- Put a drop of glue on both the clasp knot and the jump ring knot. Let the glue dry. Cut off the extra thread.

Beach Art

A Mermaid Dig a hole that's big enough for a friend to sit in comfortably. Fill the hole with sand up to her waist, which will be level with the beach.

Now make the mermaid's body. Pile some wet sand behind your friend's back and mound it into a fish shape. Make the mermaid's tail look like it's pointing straight up. To make the scales, take a large paper cup and cut away half the rim. When the rim-half is pressed into the sand, it will make a C-shape. Stagger the rows of Cs. Weave some seaweed and shells into the mermaid's hair.

Sand Art Tips

- Always work with damp sand.
- Plasterer's putty knives and wallpaper brushes make great shaping and smoothing tools.
- When making sand animals, you're better off working from a picture than from memory.

Make a Drip Castle

Fill a large bucket halfway with sand, then fill it the rest of the way with water. Grab a handful of the wet sand and let it drip onto the area where you want your castle to be.

Rock Sculptures

Use rocks and other found materials to make your own outdoor sculptures. The tricky part is getting the arrangement to balance.

Sending Beach Messages to Low-Flying Aircraft

Write a message in letters big enough (think HUGE) to be seen from way up high.

HI UP THERE!
FEEL FREE TO
SEND DOWN
SOME SNACKS

Backyard Sundial

Find a pole about 2" wide and 4' long. You may have to go to a lumber yard. Sharpen one end and stick the pole in the ground in a sunny spot. Next, nail a smooth board, about 8" square, onto the top of the pole. Using a good strong glue, attach a wooden chopstick upright at the center of the board. A knitting needle will also work very well—hammer it gently into place.

Clock Numerals

Sometimes, clocks use Roman numerals for figures. Here's how to translate the Roman numerals into modern numbers, and vice-versa:

I	II	III	IV	V	VI	VII	VIII	IX	X	XI	XII
1	2	3	4	5	6	7	8	9	10	11	12

When the sun is out and shining, you can begin marking your clock. Start in the morning. Using a watch or clock, see where the needle or chopstick or whatever you use casts its shadow at 9 A.M. Make a mark where the shadow ends, and write the number 9—or IX, if you're using Roman numerals (see the chart, previous page). Do this every hour, as long as there's enough sun for the chopstick or needle to cast a shadow.

A Few Common Sundial Inscriptions

Time and tide tarry for no man. *Tempus fugit.* (Time flies.) *Sic transit gloria mundi.* (Thus passes the glory of the world.)

Winter-Time Fun

Snowman Building Tips

■ The bottom ball is twice as wide as the middle ball, and the middle ball is twice as wide as the top ball.

■ Pour water over your snowman before you go to bed so it will have a coating of ice and stay around longer.

Snow Fort

Snow forts are great because they give you a place to hide and they also help defend you against snowball attacks.

Make of bunch of great big snowballs and roll them over to your building area. Arrange the first layer of snowballs in a circle, leaving room for a door. Now you're ready to add the next layer of snowballs. Don't put the snowballs right on top of each other—stagger them, the way a bricklayer does when building a wall.

Keep layering the snowballs until your fort is as tall as you like.

You can make windows by leaving a space, then putting a board over the top to continue stacking the snowballs.

Use branches or plywood boards for the roof. Pine boughs crisscrossed work very nicely. Pile snow on top of the boards or branches to hold them down. Make sure all your boards are strong enough to support the snow—including window boards, if you use them.

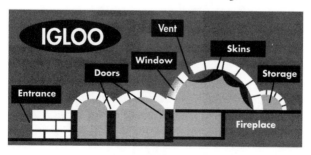

Floor Plan for a Real Igloo

Animal Tracks to Look for in the Snow.

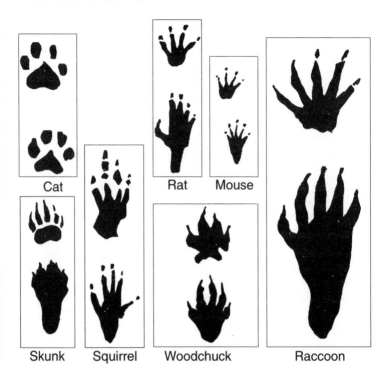

Cat

Rat

Mouse

Skunk

Squirrel

Woodchuck

Raccoon

Maple Syrup Ice Cream

There isn't any cream in this, but it tastes like ice cream!

Pour some maple syrup on a thick layer of freshly fallen snow. The syrup will freeze and turn solid. Pick up the syrup and eat it quickly, before it melts.

Backyard Skating Rink

If you have freezing, or below, temperatures and a level backyard, this is easy and fun. Later in the day, toward evening, is the best time to make your rink.

Shovel all the snow in the backyard against the fence to make sides for the rink. Get a garden hose, adjust the nozzle to make a fine spray, then spray the shoveled area with water.

The trick is to make thin layers of ice, one layer at a time. Don't make puddles. Work methodically, across and back again, to make each layer.

Be patient—it's worth it.

Camping & Campcraft

How to Pitch a Tent

■ First, practice indoors. Invite your friends over for an indoors campout. The more familiar you are with how to pitch your tent, the easier it will be when you have to do it outside in the wilderness.

■ Find the right location. Your tent site should be on a level surface, with plenty of clear space around all sides of the tent.

■ Watch for water. Don't pitch your tent right next to a stream bed or where run-off will flood you if it should start to rain.

■ Keep the floor dry. Most tents come with a built-in ground cover. If yours doesn't, make sure to use one.

Useful Knots

The very best way to learn to tie a knot is probably to join the Girl Scouts. The next, is to have a Girl Scout show you. Otherwise, study these pictures and practice, practice, practice!

■ **Over Hand** A finishing knot

■ **Square Knot** Good for tying two strings or ropes together

■ **Clove Hitch** A good knot for lashing or tying ropes to posts

■ **Two Half Hitches** Also good for tying things to posts (a horse to a hitching post, for example)

Nature Scavenger Hunt

This is a variation on a standard scavenger hunt—except all the items to be found are natural, not man-made.

For example, you could have the players find a piece of quartz, a bird feather, a clover leaf, a maple leaf, a wild onion (if it's spring)—a mixture of hard and easy to find objects. The list will depend on where you live and the time of year.

Learn What These Plants Look Like, and Then Avoid Them!

Poison Ivy

Poison Oak

Poison Sumac

Trail Signs

Trail signs were used by Native Americans to help them find their way back home or so that other Indians could follow them. Explorers, scouts, trappers, and hunters later adopted these same Indian trail signs or developed their own. After a while, the signs became more or less standardized. Here are some standard trail signs:

Branch: This Is Trail

Branch: Turn Left

Branch: Turn Right

Danger

Pebble: This Is Trail

Pebble: Turn Left

Pebble: Turn Right

Rock: This Is Trail

Rock: Turn Left

Rock: Turn Right

Sticks: This Is Trail

Sticks: Turn Left

Sticks: Turn Right

How to Play Hares and Hounds

Half the group are hounds and the other half hares. The hares start out about half an hour before the hounds. The hares mark their trail using trail signs. Thirty minutes later, the hounds set out after the hares, using the signs to track them down. It's a good idea for the hares to have lunch or dessert waiting for the whole group—that way the hounds have a real incentive to find them and won't give up!

Finding Your Way

How to find your direction:

■ **Compass** Hold the compass flat. Make sure it isn't near any metal objects, including other compasses. Always take two readings.

■ **Sun** You're facing north if (1) it's morning and the sun is shining over your right shoulder, and (2) it's afternoon and the sun is shining over your left shoulder. If you're facing north, it follows that your right hand is pointing east and your left hand, west.

■ **Stars** Find the Big Dipper. The two stars farthest from the handle (the outside edge of the Dipper) point directly to the North Star, also known as Polaris.

Make a line straight down from Polaris to the horizon—that point is directly north.

Finding Your Direction Without a Compass

■ **Moss generally grows longest on the north side of trees.** (The north side gets the least sun and stays damp longest.) But not always. Sometimes trees are shaded on the south and moss can grow on a different side, or even all around a tree. However, in a heavily wooded area, moss is usually thickest on the north or northwest.

- **Evergreen tree needle tips,** especially hemlocks, generally curve toward the east.

- **Prickly lettuce** (Lactuca scariola) has leaves that grow vertically from the stem. Those leaves point south and north.

- **Goldenrod** If you find an open field of goldenrod, the blossom tips usually point east.

- **If you have a watch with an hour hand** and it's standard, not daylight-saving, time, here's a neat trick: Hold your watch flat in your hand and point the hour hand right at the sun. South will be halfway between 12 on the watch and the hour hand. This only works north of the equator, though. If you're south of the equator (like in Australia), just reverse the directions.

- **At night, look for the North Star.** Find the Big Dipper. The two stars that make up the outer side of its cup are the pointer stars. Draw an imaginary line from the pointer stars directly to the North Star, or Polaris. It's not a real bright star. But it's the one that you'll come to if you draw that imaginary line. The point on the horizon right below the North Star is due north.

If you're having trouble finding the Big Dipper, see if you can find W-shaped Cassiopeia. Cassiopeia and the Big Dipper are the same distance from the North Star, but on opposite sides.

- **If you're lost. . . .** Stay put and make noise or signals until you're found. If you have to walk to get to safety, always walk downhill. If you find a stream, follow it. Eventually, all streams lead to civilization.

Night Walks

Get a group of friends together and go for a night walk. Everyone should bring a flashlight. You can explore your own neighborhood or you can do some stargazing. Bring some star maps and try to pick out some constellations.

What to Pack for Summer Camp

Here's what one girl, who has gone to camp every summer since she was seven, packs every year:

- 6 pairs of (mixed) denim, khaki, and mesh shorts
- 2 or 3 bathing suits
- 7 big t-shirts
- 2 pairs of long jeans
- 2 long-sleeved shirts
- 7 pairs of underpants
- 15 pairs of socks (all the same color)
- 6 sweatshirts
- 5 baseball caps
- 1 rain jacket
- 1 varsity jacket
- 1 pair of sneakers
- 1 pair of hiking boots
- 1 pair of rain boots
- 2 toothbrushes
- 2 hairbrushes
- Bug spray
- Sunscreen
- Shampoo
- Lots of food—the kind that keeps.

9. Animals & Plants

How to Adopt a Kitten

Visit the local animal shelter. There are many lost and homeless animals there, including many cats and kittens. Pick one you like.

■ **Spay or neuter your cat.** The shelter may offer to do this as a part of the adoption process. By having your kitten spayed (if she's a female) or neutered (if he's a male), you will help prevent the overpopulation of cats. The reason animals are in shelters is that there are too many for people to take care of.

■ **Get shots for the kitten.** Kittens need to have shots, such as distemper, to help them fight off diseases.

■ **Make the kitten a place of her own.** When you get the kitten home, allow her some time in a small room—perhaps the bathroom—to get used to living with you. A kitten needs to recognize the sights, sounds, and smells of its new home. Even though the new kitten is very cute, try not to pick her up a lot for the first day or two. Give her a small toy to play with—a spool, maybe, or a ball.

■ **Show her the litter box.** Kittens need to be shown where the litter box is. Place the litter box on the other side of the room from her food and water, and place the kitten in the litter box. She'll get the idea.

■ **Food and water.** Kittens need plenty of fresh, clean water to drink. As for food, you may want to start your kitten on food specially prepared for baby cats. Dry food is okay; in fact, that's probably what the shelter was feeding her, so she'll be used to it. If you give her canned food or special foods, you may have a difficult time later trying to get her to eat dry food, which is much cheaper (and smells better!).

Horse Sense

How to Approach a Horse You can make a bad impression on a horse, just like you can on a person. Do *not* run up to the horse and begin patting it on the nose or shoving food at it. Under no circumstances should you ever walk up *behind* a horse! Approach the horse slowly from one side while speaking its name. Get close enough for the horse to see and smell you, then slowly raise one hand and gently stroke its neck. If you've brought a treat (like an apple or carrot) hold it in your open hand and let the horse take it from you. If you treat the horse like a shy stranger, not a dumb animal, you just may make a friend for life.

To learn more about horses, you can write to the following organizations:

The American Youth Horse Council
4093 Ironworks Pike
Lexington, KY 40511
1-800-Try-AYHC
(They publish a horse industry handbook. Call or write for information.)

North American Riding for the Handicapped Association
P.O. Box 33150
Denver, CO 80233

American Horse Shows Association
220 E. 42nd St. Suite 409
New York, NY 10017-5809
(They have a rider's guide. Write to them for information.)

To get a horse charm, along with a pamphlet, send $1.00 to:
Horse Source
Dept. FS
637 Meadows Drive
Wenatchee, WA 98801

Indoor Horseshow

Set up an obstacle course in your living room and put a toy horse through its paces, or pretend you are the horse: make fences from overturned boxes or chairs and have your horse jump them. Turn a blue towel into a pond for a water jump. Line up some mops and brooms for trotting poles. You can make other obstacles from things around the house. If you're playing with friends, make up some ribbons. You or one of your friends can be the judge, and award blue, red, and yellow ribbons for best jumper, best of show, etc.

How to Saddle a Horse

Saddling a horse is not a difficult process. There are only two variables that will affect how the job is done. One is the confidence of the girl doing the job. The other is the nervousness of the horse.

■ **Tie him** Horses will walk away while you're saddling them unless they are restrained. Attach a lead rope to his halter and tie the rope to a post.

■ **Brush him down.** A horse's idea of fun is to roll in the dirt, and a little piece of gravel in the middle of his back can mean a big headache if you pile a saddle and a big girl on top of it.

■ **Stand on the left.** Do most of your work from the horse's left side. When horses are broken, this is part of their training. When you have to go around behind a horse, keep your hand on him as you walk, or pass far enough behind him that he won't be startled. Talk or whistle—but let him know where you are. Horses hate surprises. Unfortunately, almost anything will surprise a horse.

■ **Put on the saddle blanket.** Place the pad or blanket above the withers on the neck and slide it back into position, centered, with the front edge right at the peak of the withers. This smoothes the hair under the blanket. If the blanket is large enough to fold, the fold should be in the front.

■ **Buckle up.** Place the saddle on the horse's back so the front edge is just above the front edge of the saddle pad. Common mistake: Placing the saddle too far back. The seat belt on a saddle doesn't keep you in the seat, it keeps the seat on the horse. It's called the *cinch belt*, and it's the thing hanging down that isn't a stirrup. Working from the horse's left, reach under, grab the cinch and bring it up and through the saddle's D-ring, then back through the cinch ring, then up again to secure it. Some cinch belts tie, some buckle. How tight? Not too; just snug it in place (you'll tighten it later). There should be enough room to comfortably squeeze a couple of fingers beneath the belt, but not enough room for your whole hand. If you immediately tighten the belt, you may startle the horse.

■ **Feel for fit.** Let the animal get used to the feel of the saddle. You do the same. Adjust it and make sure it feels like it's in place and secure. If the saddle has a chest band, belt it in place now.

■ **Bridle stuff:** Keep the horse restrained by placing the reins around his neck. (You can also slip the halter down until it clears his nose, then bring it back up so it forms a loop around his neck.) Holding the bit in your left hand and the headstall in your right, slide the bit into he horse's mouth and bring the headstall over his ears. If he won't say "Ah," slide a finger into the corner of his mouth; there are no choppers there, and he'll open wide for you.

■ **Ride.** Now tighten the cinch so it's secure, and mount from the left side. Show the horse you mean to control it by directing its first movements with you on its back. If you find your feet in the stirrups, but your butt on the ground, you'll know something's amiss. Make the necessary adjustment. When the ride's over, reverse the entire process and brush down the horse. If he's hot, walk him until his breathing slows. Don't let an overheated horse drink more than a handful of water.

How to Draw a Horse

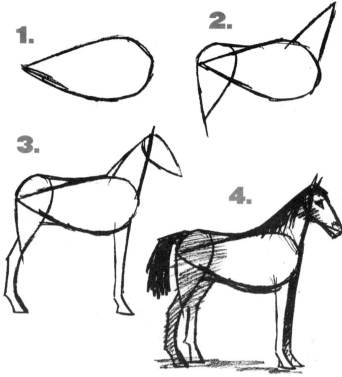

1.

2.

3.

4.

The Points of a Horse

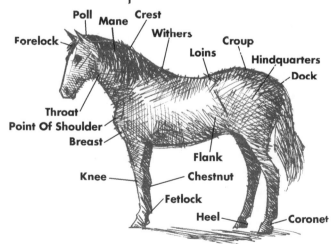

Poll · Mane · Crest · Withers · Croup · Loins · Hindquarters · Dock

Forelock

Throat · Point Of Shoulder · Breast · Flank

Knee · Chestnut

Fetlock · Heel · Coronet

If you have a goldfish . . .

Don't change all the water at once! Change a little each time—never more than a third of the bowl. **Don't** overfeed her! **Don't** tap on the side of her tank! This makes a *huge racket* inside and can make the fish so insane that it will die.

U-Catch-'Em Pets

Amphibians and reptiles can make interesting pets. Even better, you can catch them yourself. The best time of the year to collect them is spring. Try collecting at night, too, after it's dark—bring a flashlight! One of the best ways to learn about reptiles and amphibians is to "borrow" one for a while. But if you do, make sure you return it to its home in one piece. Also, don't be a homewrecker: leave your creature's habitat in the same condition you found it!

Catching Lizards: Lizards are cold-blooded, which means they need to be warmed by the sun before they can go about their lizard business. Their scales work like solar heating panels. When they bask, they're really collecting and storing solar energy, to use later.

Because lizards are sluggish in the in the morning, that's the best time to catch one. Move toward it very slowly, as it basks. Pick the lizard up by the back of its neck. If you grab a lizard by its tail, the tail will fall off and thrash around for several minutes. This is a lizard's natural defense against its predators. Although the lizard will eventually grow a new tail, it's not a good idea to go around pulling off their tails: lizards are more vulnerable to predators (and less attractive to mates) without their tails.

Snakes: Obviously, you need to know a little about the different snakes in your area before you start catching them. Most snakes are harmless to humans, but not all! Learn about your local snake population from the library or Parks Department in your town. Like lizards, snakes are cold-blooded (as are all reptiles). Morning and sundown are the best times to go snake-hunting. Once you've determined that a snake is harmless, you can catch it by stepping very gently on its 'neck'. Reach down and pick it up behind its head.

Salamanders, newts and efts: These creatures "drink" water by absorbing it through their porous skin. They need to stay in dark, moist places to survive. The best place to find one is under a log or the branch of a fallen tree. When you lift the log, be sure to replace it gently: a whole universe of creatures make their home in the decaying wood. Always wet your hand, before picking up newts—your 98.6° dry hand feels like a hot oven to them. Also, don't hold on to them too long—they'll die if their skin dries out.

Catching a Doodlebug

Lots of insects make their homes in the ground. When they burrow they bring the displaced dirt up to the surface. If you look closely, you'll see the entrances to these underground tunnels; they look somewhat like miniature volcanoes. You can stick a long blade of grass down one the volcano holes. Sometimes a lion beetle, or "doodlebug" will be clinging to the grass when you pull it back up! Study it for a bit, then let it go back home.

Warning: Some wasps burrow into the ground, too. Steer clear of them!

Capturing Tips

Bring a container with plenty of air holes.

Once you get your new pets home, they'll need homes of their own. Glass terrariums (available at pet stores) can be adapted to whatever environment you need:

■ **Salamanders** require lots of water, some dry land, and some green plants.
■ **Frogs, tadpoles and turtles** should be in a semi-aquarium: lots of water, a little bit of land.

- **Snakes** will need a cage.
- **Spiders** are easy to catch.

What Do They Eat?

- **Frogs, salamanders, and lizards:** Insects with soft bodies and very small worms
- **Tadpoles:** Water plants and cornmeal
- **Snakes:** Chopped up raw meat or fish, mice, and small-ish eggs

Wild Birds as Pets

You don't want to catch them and put them inside, because they'll die. But you can still make pets out of them, even though they're wild. The easiest way to make friends with birds is to feed them.

Not every bird flies south in the wintertime, and sometimes pickings can be slim for those who stay behind. The birds will thank you if you pick out a special tree and keep it well stocked with goodies. (Choose a tree that usually attracts a lot of birds.) Every year at Longwood Gardens in Kennet Square, Pennsylvania, a "wildlife tree" is decorated for the local birds and other woodland creatures. Here are a few of their ornaments:

Pinecone Treat

Wrap some string around the top (apical end) of a pinecone, leaving enough string to be tied for a hanger. With a blunt knife, spread peanut butter over the pinecone and roll it in birdseed.

Grapefruit Cups

Take all of the sections and pulp out of a grapefruit half. With a pencil (or the end of a small paintbrush) poke three evenly-spaced holes near the rim of the grapefruit. Also, poke one hole in the bottom of the cup, for drainage. Let it dry out for a day or two. String three lengths of yarn or raffia through the three holes and tie them together at the top, for hanging. Fill the grapefruit bowl with birdseed, popcorn, or raisins.

Cranberry & Cheerios Garland

Using a sturdy needle and dental floss, string cranberries and plain (not sweetened) Cheerios to make a garland. You should string the thread through the top and bottom of each berry—not the sides. Drape the garland on a tree.

Bird Donuts

In a mixing bowl, combine:

- 1 cup birdseed
- A handful of unpopped popcorn
- $1/2$ cup of coarse cornmeal
- A handful of unsweetened dry cereal (Cheerios, oatmeal, Rice Krispies, etc.)
- $1/2$ cup of crunchy peanut butter

Mix the ingredients together with your hands. Shape the mixture into small patties. With your thumb, make a hole in the middle of each patty. Bake in a slow (250°) oven for 45 minutes. Cool, and string yarn through the hole.

Suet Bags

Like humans, birds need fats for energy—and to keep their feathers sleek and waterproof. Most of the fat they need comes from nut and seed oils, but beef fat (suet) is a welcome addition to their winter diet. You can get a chunk of suet from a butcher or the meat department of your supermarket. Place the suet in a net bag (the kind that onions come in) and tie it with a piece of string. Hang the bag near a branch where birds can land.

Indian Corn

Tie string or raffia around the top of one large (or three small) ears of corn. Tie at the top and hang it on your tree.

Crabapple Bundle

Take a 15" length of florist's wire and push one end of it through the top of a crabapple. Try to keep the wire as close to the center as possible. Bend a hook at the end of the wire and stick it back into the base of the first apple. Take another crabapple and do the same with the other end of your wire. Bend the wire at its center and hang the two apples over a tree branch.

After the birds have taken away the food, leave your strings on the tree. They'll be looking for nest-building material in the spring!

Bird Nest Building

Try this in the spring when birds are nesting:

Find a net bag, the kind oranges or onions come in, and fill it with different materials a bird might use when building its nest—leaves, short lengths of string and yarn, hair, feathers, twigs, dried grass, straw, small scraps of cloth—use your imagination! Let the different materials stick out from the bag so the birds can get at them easily.

Tie the bag to a tree branch. Find a spot where you can observe the birds.

Coconut Bird Feeder

You will need:

- A coconut
- A large nail or awl
- A hammer
- A coping saw or hacksaw
- Some heavy-duty string or rope
- An eye-hole screw

Pick out a large, ripe coconut. Drain the liquid out of it by hammering a nail or awl into one of the (lengthwise) ends of the coconut. Place the coconut on a old, folded towel to keep it from splitting while you make holes. Turn coconut over to the opposite end and make another hole. This will be the pilot hole for your hanger.

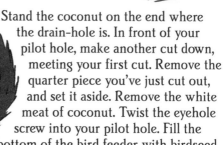

First Cut

Holding the coconut with one hand, cut halfway down the middle with the coping saw. (You may need some help here.)

Eyehole Screw

Second Cut

Stand the coconut on the end where the drain-hole is. In front of your pilot hole, make another cut down, meeting your first cut. Remove the quarter piece you've just cut out, and set it aside. Remove the white meat of coconut. Twist the eyehole screw into your pilot hole. Fill the bottom of the bird feeder with birdseed and hang it from a tree branch.

The Topography of a Bird

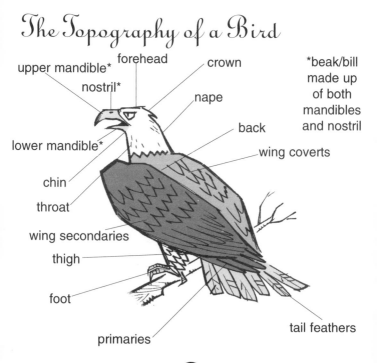

upper mandible*
forehead
crown
nostril*
nape
lower mandible*
back
wing coverts
chin
throat
wing secondaries
thigh
foot
primaries
tail feathers

*beak/bill made up of both mandibles and nostril

Be a Field Biologist

Biologists—scientists who study living organisms—are constantly learning new things about our environment. You can help them, by picking an area in your neighborhood (a park, a field, or a vacant lot) and becoming the world's greatest authority on that particular place. Begin by giving it a great name, if it doesn't already have one. Next, make a map (see "Map Making," page 177). Draw in all the natural features (trees, creeks, hills, and rock outcroppings) along with some of the manmade ones.

Keep a record. One of the most important things a scientist does is to make repeated experiments and keep a careful record of the results. For instance, you could do a study of the birds in your area. With a compass in one hand and a pen in the other, sit quietly in your study area and watch the flightlines of passing birds for exactly one-half hour. Using a field guidebook, do your best to identify the species. After noting the date, time, temperature, and weather conditions of this particular observation, write down the direction they're flying, and keep notes on their behavior in your study area. Are they singing? Chasing after one another? Foraging for food? Once you have this information, the important thing is to repeat this same experiment at other times throughout the year. When you've collected a year's worth of data, you might want to contact your local Parks Department or Audubon Society. Chances are, someone will be interested in all your hard work. You can do these kinds of experiments observing plants, insects, or woodland mammals (squirrels, chipmunks, etc.). You can even observe the behavior of the humans who share this piece of ground.

You could become the world's greatest expert on your particular study spot. Someday, someone may want to build a brand new mall in your study area. Your research might be invaluable in helping people to make the best possible decisions. If you enjoy this kind of research, there are many exciting jobs—studying toucans in the Amazon Basin or polar bears in arctic Alaska— that could take you all over the world!

Get in touch with the National Geographic Society, National Audubon Society, or your local Department of Fish and Game.

Different Kinds of Farms You Can Make

Butterfly Farm

■ **Find a caterpillar.** Use an insect or butterfly book to identify it and find out what he/she eats. The bush or leaf you discovered your crawler on is a pretty big hint!

■ **Keep your caterpillar in a jar,** with a few small holes poked in the lid. Every day open the lid a couple of times and sprinkle water on the leaves to keep them moist. If the leaves start to whither, replace them. Also, lean a stick against the inside of the jar so the caterpillar can climb up it and, eventually, make a chrysalis.

■ **Once the caterpillar does make a chrysalis,** wait and watch. When the butterfly does emerge from the chrysalis, take a picture while it's drying its wings. Then let it go. Unless, of course, you want to mount your butterfly as part of collection.

How to Make a Killing Jar

Not as cruel as it sounds, a killing jar is what lepidopterists (moth and butterfly enthusiasts) use to kill their specimens quickly and painlessly.

Put a few drops of ethyl acetate (available from a biological supply store) on a piece of cotton at the bottom of an airtight jar. Next, put a couple of layers of paper towels on top. Put the butterfly in the jar.

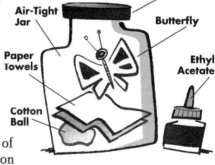

Labels: Air-Tight Jar, Lid, Butterfly, Paper Towels, Ethyl Acetate, Cotton Ball

How to Mount a Butterfly

You can, of course, make your own display box, but you have to be absolutely certain it is pest free. If not, your specimens will be destroyed. Guaranteed-pest-free display cases can also be bought from biological supply stores.

Collecting Moths at Night

Do this on a night that's still (with no wind), warm, and moonless: stretch a sheet out between two poles or over a clothes line—whatever's handy. Put a black light—not an ultraviolet light—in front of the sheet. *Voilà*—moths!

You can also raise moths in the same way you raise butterflies. Moth caterpillars turn into pupas, not chrysalises, though.

Worm Farm

First, you need to find a worm hole. Look for the little balls of dirt that worms leave on their holes. Dilute some dry mustard in water (not too much; you don't want to kill them) and pour it down the hole. Wait for the worm to wiggle up. Rinse the worm off, and put it in your worm farm.

How to Make the Farm You should have a large plastic container (like the kind sweaters are stored in). Fill it with rich soil. You want to keep the soil moist, but not too wet. Every few days, put in a few large lettuce leaves and spray the leaves with water. Cover the box with a lid that has some holes in it. Worms are actually pretty fun to keep. They have lots of baby worms, and they're fun to see.

Homemade Ant Farm

■ You'll need about 100 ants, a one-quart mason jar, a shallow soup-sized bowl, and a pie tin that's bigger than the soup bowl.

■ Fill the jar and the bowl both about three fourths full (no more!) with dirt. Put the jar in the bowl and the bowl in the pie tin. Fill the pie tin with water. The water will work like a moat to keep the ants from leaving the farm.

■ Don't cover the jar.

■ Feed your ants soft fruit dipped in honey or sugary water, candy, cheese, bread, vegetables—even bits of meat. Make sure you vary their diet. Keep the pieces of food small and don't let them get moldy—take them out if that happens.

■ Every couple of days or so, add a spoonful of sugar water to the dirt. Don't give the ants too much water, though!

You should see your first tunnels after a few days.

Gathering Ants

Look for small mounds of dry soil or sand—ants should be nearby. When you see an ant, hold out a pencil or stick. Let the ant crawl onto it and then gently tap the ant into your dirt-filled jar.

Worker ants live about six weeks, so that's how long you can hope to keep your farm going—unless you're lucky enough to get a queen!

Grow a Green Thumb!

A Family Garden

Here's a fun way to make vegetables taste great: grow your own!

Gardens should be planned before they are planted. Start by taking a piece of graph paper and making a small map of your new garden. Draw a rectangle that represents the shape of the garden, then start "planting" your crops by blocking out areas where they will go inside the rectangle.

■ **Put all the perennial plants**—including asparagus, rhubarb, and flowers—along one edge so they won't get in the way of the yearly maintenance of the garden.

■ **Plant corn** along another edge. You need at least three rows of corn to make sure cross pollination takes place. One long row won't work. Corn and other tall plants should go along the northern edge, if possible, and shorter plants should go along the southern edge.

■ **Don't plant too many tomatoes!** They grow like crazy and wham! They all show up at once and you're eating tomatoes until your turn into walking catsup. Same thing with zucchini, except for the catsup part.

■ **Make room** to work between the rows of vegetables.

■ **Let Nature help.** Here are some vegetable-couples—pairs of plants that do well when planted next to each other, either alternately or in paired rows:

- Beans, Celery
- Cucumbers, Corn
- Onions, Radishes
- Peppers, Basil
- Tomatoes, Marigolds
- Carrots, Beets
- Lettuce, Potatoes
- Peas, Turnips
- Potatoes, Beans

■ **Now, wait** until the last frost and take your garden map outside and start planting!

How to make a scarecrow

■ Nail two boards together in an cross shape, with one board much longer than the other.

■ Get an old pair of pants and slip one leg through the long board. Put an old shirt on over the "arms." Tuck the shirt inside the pants and tie them together with a rope.

■ Stuff the body with leaves or straw.

■ Stuff an old pillowcase for the head. Tie it off, stick it on the top of the pole, and tuck it into the shirt. Draw a face on with a marker. If you want to get fancy, you can sew on button features, but do that before you stick it on the pole.

■ Hats and gloves (stuff them!) are nice touches, but not necessary. If you tie tin pie plates on the arms, the clatter might help to scare away the birds.

Planning a Flower Garden

Call Burpee Gardens (1-800-888-1447) and ask them to send you their free catalog. They sell flower garden kits, which include a selection of seeds, plant markers, a garden plan, and planting instructions. There are kits for sun-loving flowers, shade-loving flowers, perennials (plants that grow year after year), and annuals (plants that flower, then die over the winter).

A Forced Bulb

These are great gifts to make or sell in late winter.

You'll need:

■ Hyacinth bulbs—one for each gift. Buy your bulbs in the fall.

■ A clear glass jar with an opening a little smaller than the width of your bulb. Dijon mustard jars are ideal.

■Ribbon

Buy your bulbs in the fall and keep them in a paper bag in the refrigerator until you're ready to start forcing them. It's called "forcing" because when you take your bulb out of the refrigerator, you trick it into thinking that spring has arrived. In nature, bulbs don't begin sending out roots until the ground thaws—usually in March. Bulbs need to "rest" for at least six weeks before they can send up new shoots. This resting time is called a *dormant* period.

Take the bulbs out three weeks to a month before you plan on giving or selling them. Fill the glass jar with water and place the bulb on top of it, with the root end down.

The root end looks a little bumpy, whereas the shoot end is pointed, like an onion—which is also a bulb.

The root buds should just touch the water. Put the bulb in a cool, dark place (not the refrigerator) and add a little water to the jar every day or so, to replace the water that evaporates. Once a week, change the water. Within a week you should see the root tips begin growing down. Soon you'll see a white shoot forcing its way up through the papery skin of the bulb.

When both the roots and the shoot are an inch long, take the bulb out and place it in a bright place—but not in direct sunlight. The white shoot will turn green and in a week or two you'll see a flower beginning to form inside its green tip. When the first bloom appears, tie a beautiful ribbon around the neck of the jar and give it to someone special. Everybody loves to get a living flower—especially when it reminds them that spring is just around the corner!

You Can Force Fruits and Vegetables, Too

Cut off the top of a carrot or pineapple and place it in a shallow dish with a little water. The leafy green part will begin to grow and your carrot or pineapple will start to send out roots. Change the water often to keep your plant from getting moldy.

More Growing Things

These make good gifts, too.

Re-potted Herbs At a nursery, buy a starter pack of different "kitchen" herbs— basil, thyme, rosemary, chives, oregano, mint, etc. Buy some 3" clay flowerpots and a small bag of soil. Take each plant out of its plastic cell and repot it into a clay flower pot. To repot, put a spoonful of soil in a flower pot, set the herb in the middle and fill in with more soil. Tie a ribbon around each plant, and give your herbs away as gifts.

An Herb Garden Plant several different herbs together in a large round flowerpot or a small planter.

A Salad Garden From a nursery, buy several different kinds of lettuce in starter packs. Put the lettuces together in a large flowerpot or small wooden box. Give with a bottle of gourmet salad dressing.

A Plant Kit Put together a small flowerpot, a package of seeds and a Ziplok bag, filled with planting soil. Write growing instructions on an index or recipe card. Put your plant kit in a box, and wrap.

A Fund-Raising Idea

Re-potted plants and plant kits are great fund-raising items, too. Figure out the cost of each unit by adding up all your expenses and dividing that number by the total number of units. To get the selling price, double your cost.

Acknowledgments

Following is a list of the names of all the kids (and grown-ups) who gave us the stuff for both *A Girl's Guide to Life* and *A Boy's Guide to Life.* We are grateful to them all, each and every one.

If you know something fun or useful you think other boys ought to know, please send it to us. We'd like to include it—and your name—in our newsletter or in the next guide! Our address is:

Kids Life
116 West Jefferson St.
Mankato, KS 66956

Our phone number is (800) 394-4984.

Or you can visit us on the World Wide Web! Kids Life is at

http://www.kidslife.com

Thanks!

P.S.—If you've got a brother, he might like to read *A Boy's Guide to Life.* Just an idea.

Contributors

Brady Alexander
Cortney Alexander
Jazmin Alfonseca
Alex Anders
Marissa Arciola
Erica Arneson
Lauren Arneson
Mikal Baker
Arne Bakker
Philip Bannerman
Reuben Bannon
Gabriella Baum
Sabrina Baum
Drew H. Benton
Toby Black
Laura Blinkhorn
Susanna Bonam
Bonnie Bowser
Ashley Boyles
April R. Boyles
Brett Boyles
Denis Boyles

Evan Boyles
Hattie Boyles
Maggie Boyles
Marilyn Boyles
Nathan Boyles
Stuart Boyles
Travis Boyles
Whitney Boyles
Len Brantner
Ian Brodie
Dylan Brooks
Rebecca B. Brown
Sam Burrows
Ellis Caase
John Carlucci
Alonzo Carnozzo
Tessa Carnozzo
Larry Cassana
Penn Chamson
Andy Charlton
Sam Charlton
Christina Ciprian-Matthews

Dean Clayton
Amanda Clement
Bill Clifton
Pedar Craine
Jeremy Crouse
Elisa Dandrew
Miles Dandrew
Bob Davis
Lynda Deschler
Keith Dibert
Hank Dogget
Tom Downey
Stephen Duffy
Sarita Patrice Dunn
Ry Eiderman
Bill Englund
Shadisha Eubanks
Letizia Figg
Troy Figueroa
Dotsie Filanowska
F. Scott Fitzgerald
Joshua Force

Hillary Franck
Ursula Frenche
James Pierce Friedman
Charles Fry
Conor Gallagher
John Gallagher
Tavish Gallagher
Jake Gardner
Peter Garibaldi
Darren Garman
Marcus Garruba
Francesca Gioeli
Ryan Gioeli
Chelsea Gisando
Ajana Grantham
Aisha Gray
Melissa Guadalupe
Michelle Guadalupe
Greg Guttfield
Jason Hall
Terry Hall
Alan Hammer

Craig Hammer
Curtis Harper
Arno Harris
Ronell Henderson
Angelo Hennessey
Ariel Hensley
Max Hensley
Nathaniel Heubscher
Monk Hooper
Duke Hoover
Indiana Hoover
Texas Hoover
Olivia Horne
Frank Horvath
Jonas Howitte
David Donaghy Isler
Edmund Donaghy Isler
Tonya Israel
Karen Jameson
Ben Jervis
Charles Johannson
Georg Kajanus
Vinz Kamfritt
Megan Kelly
Susannah Kelly
Michael Kennedy
Johanna Kisimu
Peter Kunze
John Lardas
Lawrence Laskey
Stan Leach
Jeff Leader
Amie A. Lewis
Kevin Liang
Arye Lipman
Blaise Lipman
Danielle Litt
Kirsten Loderer
Heather Macrae
Kaitlin Macrae
Julia Madden

Melissa Magazine
Tristan Mantell-Hoffmann
Yves Manton
Jasmine Edith Marin
Fis Masterson
Norman Mazzarri
Charles McKinney
Patrice Metcalf-Putnam
Carly Moretti
Gillian Morgan
Honor Morgan
Andrew Morganstern
Tammy Mulford
Jordan Nassar
Jerry Neele
Max Newman
Rebecca Newman
Kris Ney
Alex Nixon
Marie Norris
Erin O'Brien
Wyatt Lowenstein O'Day
Hen O'Rourke
Natassia Ocasio
Frank Oliver
Richard Olivier
Steve Parin
Timothy Paterno
Brian Paul
Sanford Penn-Riles
Gary Pensance
Elvis Perrine
Caroline Pohlmann
Jon Robert Pohlmann
Rosina Pohlmann
Susan Pohlmann
Nora Prentice
Megan Raelson

Joey Randazzo
Madeline Weiss Randazzo
Curtis Reinking
Ethan Reinking
Joshua Reinking
Andy Renwick
Phil Rizzuto
Devan Robbins
Kelly Rodriques
Morgan Ross
Noah Ross
Nicole Ross
Sarah Ruane
Charles Ryland
Gretchen Salisbury
Yvette Sallay
Will Samuelson
Jackson Sansoucie
Kaitlin Sansoucie
Artemis Seay
Hector Seay
Elaine Seggerman
Jeffrey Shane
Daniel Shaw
Michael Shayne
Stuart Sherwin
Ajit Singh
Angela Sinicropi
Jamie Stack
Karen Stack
Suzanna Stack
Tim Stanton
Alice Starr
Benjamin Starr
Lisa Starr
Gregg Stebben
Peter Steers
Charlie Stein
Harry Stein
Sadie Stein
Hallie Steiner
Banner Stephens
Dan Stephens

Lenny Stetler
Elizabeth Stotler-Turner
Reuvie Sunshine
Hannah Sunshne
Tom Szody
Martin Takigawa
Chas Taylor
Matt Taylor
Sam Taylor
Shawnna Thomas
Matthew Torres
Alexandra Townsend
Rachel Townsend
Scott Townsend
Kathy Traynor
John Tubb-Tasker
Larry Turner
Priscilla Turner
Whitney Turner
Mark Twain
Philip Tzevelis
Rand Ulrich
Selino Valdes
Catherine Vasserman
Lucy Vasserman
Aili Venho
Clifford Venho
Mollie Vosick-Levinson
Simon Vozick-Levinson
Siddequa Walker
David Weir
Gregory Weir
Jonah White
Steve Wiener
Jamal Wilkes
Dave Wilson
Anna Zamm
Tim Zimmer
Dave Zincko